Student Name: _____

The Virginia Experience™

For Fourth Graders and Fifth Grade Review

Student Workbook

Written by
Carole Marsh

Editorial Assistants: Brenda Crowley, Danielle Omans & Diana Phillips
Art & Design: Steven Saint-Laurent & Cecil Anderson

©2000 Carole Marsh/Gallopade International. All Rights Reserved.

No part of this publication may be reproduced in whole or in part, stored in a retrieval system, or transmitted in any form or by any means, electronic, mechanical, photocopying, recording or otherwise, without written permission from the publisher.

~ This book is not reproducible. ~

The Virginia Experience Team

Carole Marsh & Bob Longmeyer — Research/Writing

 **Michael Marsh** — Website Design

 **Michele Yother** — President

 Jamie Squblu — Customer Service

Published by
GALLOPADE INTERNATIONAL
www.virginiaexperience.com
800-536-2GET
www.gallopade.com

 **Sherry Moss & Sue Gentzke** — Marketing

Chad Beard & Chad Morrison — Production

 Printed in the USA by McGowan Publications and Winks Printing

Brenda Crowley — Documentation & SOL Correlations

 **Steven Saint-Laurent & Cecil Anderson** — Graphic Design

 **Diana Phillips & Danielle Omans** — Editing

ISBN 0793394139
• **First Edition** •

©2000 Carole Marsh • All Rights Reserved.
No part of this publication may be reproduced in whole or in part,
stored in a retrieval system, or transmitted in any form or by any means,
electronic, mechanical, photocopying, recording or otherwise,
without written permission from the publisher.

*Gallopade is proud to be a member of these
educational organizations and associations:*

~ This book is not reproducible. ~

Carole Marsh Virginia Titles

The Virginia Experience! For Grades 3-8

The Virginia Experience! for Kindergarteners Student Workbook
The Virginia Experience! for Kindergarteners Teacher Resource Book

The Virginia Experience! for First Graders Student Workbook
The Virginia Experience! for First Graders Teacher Resource Book

The Virginia Experience! for Second Graders Student Workbook
The Virginia Experience! for Second Graders Teacher Resource Book

The Virginia Experience! for Third Graders Student Workbook
The Virginia Experience! for Third Graders Teacher Resource Book

The Virginia Experience! for Fourth Graders and Fifth Grade Review Student Workbook
The Virginia Experience! for Fourth Graders and Fifth Grade Review Teacher Resource Book

The Virginia Experience! for Seventh Graders Student Workbook
The Virginia Experience! for Seventh Graders Teacher Resource Book

The Virginia Experience! for Eleventh Graders Student Workbook
The Virginia Experience! for Eleventh Graders Teacher Resource Book

The Virginia Experience! for Twelfth Graders Student Workbook
The Virginia Experience! for Twelfth Graders Teacher Resource Book

The Virginia Experience! Standards of Learning Reference Guide

The Virginia Experience! Poster/Map

Virginia Facts & Factivities CD-ROM, Teacher's Guide, Lesson Plans, and Reproducible Activities

Virginia "BIO" Bingo Game
Virginia "GEO" Bingo Game
Virginia "HISTO" Bingo Game

State Stuff for Virginia!: 40+ Carole Marsh Virginia Books

Virginia Archives Alive
Virginia Penny Pocket Projects
Bird's Eye View Maps for Virginia
©NOW! Current Events for Virginia!

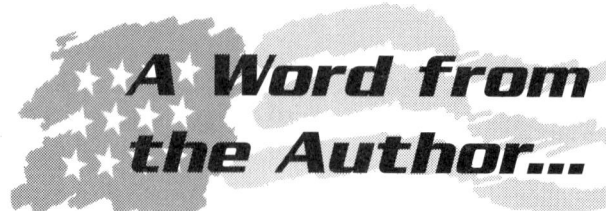

A Word from the Author...

Dear Students,

Whether you're first studying the great state of Virginia, or reviewing for your Standards of Learning test, I have a secret for you: almost everything you ever want or need to know, you can learn right in your own backyard... in your very own state!

As you progress in school, you will find that your Virginia state studies prepare you to understand people and places around the world. Why? Because you will already possess a wealth of knowledge about how things work – history, geography, politics, etc. – in a single corner of the world that you know well: your own state!

Virginia is a very special state to study. It has a history so remarkable that it is impossible to successfully study the past (or the present!) without understanding that what happened in Virginia helped create the greatest nation on earth – America! Virginia enjoys an amazing geography of incredible beauty and fascination. The state's people are unique and have accomplished many great things. When you learn about these extraordinary people, you will learn about yourself!

Almost everything about Virginia is interesting – whether that's politics, sea life, mountain heritage, surprising trivia, the arts, legend and lore – and much, much more. Even people who have long been out of school and who could read about and study any subject they desire (and who don't even have to pass a test!) are drawn to study your state – The Commonwealth of Virginia.

I have learned a lot by researching, writing, and photographing The Virginia Experience books and other products. So come along with me and enjoy your very own Virginia Experience – it's the trip of a lifetime!

Carole Marsh

Table of Contents

Icon Identification	6
Section I ~ Geography	**7**
Chapter 1	9
Chapter 2	23
Section II ~ History, Economics, and Civics	**63**
Chapter 1	65
Chapter 2	111
Chapter 3	125
Chapter 4	137
Section III ~ Extra Credit	**161**
Practice Test	169
Section IV ~ Appendix	**171**
Virginia Timeline	172
People On Parade	174
Virginia Basic Facts	180
Gazetteer	181
Geography Glossary	182
History Glossary	183
Glossary of Indian Words and Names	184
Reference Guide	185
Maps	186
Index	190
About the Author / Notes About Answer Key	192

Icon Identification

Hard-To-Believe-But-True!
Fascinating trivia!

Map Skill Builder
Learn map skills and never be lost!

Question for Discussion
Who wants to be a millionaire?!

Reading Activity
The best kind of activity!

Scavenger Hunt!
Stuff for you to look for!

Math Experience
A neat math problem or info!

Quick Quiz
Think fast!

Special Economics Info
Money Makes the World Go 'Round

Origin/Definition
Word origins or definitions.

The Great Debate
A chance to share your opinion!

Background Check
Deep digging unearthed this stuff!

Look-It-Up!
We can't give you EVERYTHING!

Enrichment
Stuff that will stick with you!

High Tech
Computer Technology Connections!

Special Civics Information

Quick Review
You didn't forget, did you?

Write About It!
A writing activity.

Scratch Pad
A place for calculations... or doodles!

One More - Just for Fun!
All work and no play...

Essential Skills
You can't live without these!

Section 1

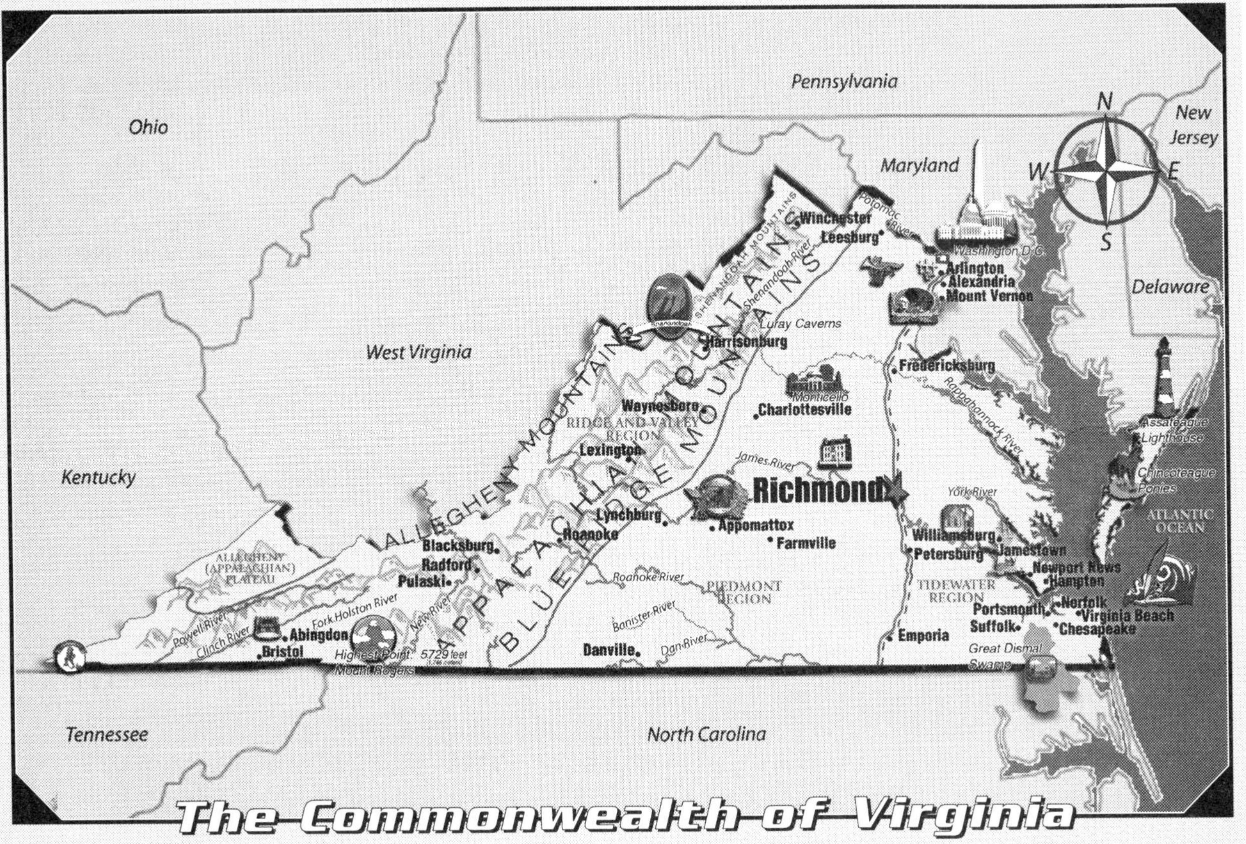

The Commonwealth of Virginia

Geography

~ This book is not reproducible. ~

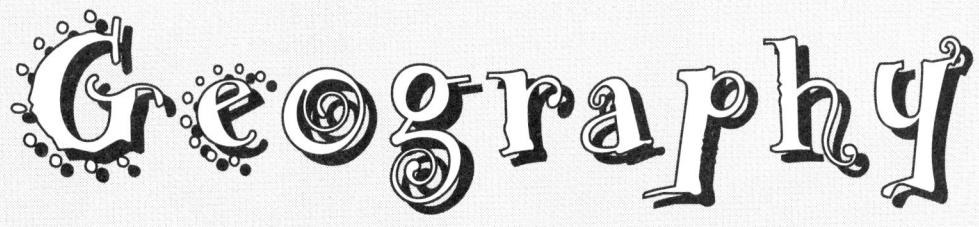

Thanks to Virginia's varied geography, visitors can enjoy the beauty of beaches, mountains, and valleys. You can hike or ski in the Blue Ridge or Allegheny Mountains, swim or sun yourself near the Atlantic Ocean, and learn about our nation's history by visiting the many historical sites around the state!

Chapter 1

Virginia is divided into these four geographic regions:

- Tidewater
- Piedmont
- Ridge & Valley
- Allegheny (Appalachian) Plateau

Geographic factors had a large impact on the expansion and development of Virginia.

4.1a - Geographic factors had a large impact on the expansion and development of Virginia.

American Indians, First on Our Land!

The American Indians were the first people who lived in Virginia. They lived in all areas of the state. There were three American Indian language groups.

Algonquian language group lived primarily in the Tidewater region. The Powhatans, who met the first settlers in Jamestown, were members of this group.

The *Siouan* language group lived primarily in the Piedmont region.

The *Iroquoian* language group lived in the Allegheny (Appalachian) Plateau. The Cherokee were a part of this group.

1. Write **I** on the region where the Iroquoian language group lived.
2. Write **S** on the region where the Siouan language group lived.
3. Write **A** on the region where the Algonquian language group lived.

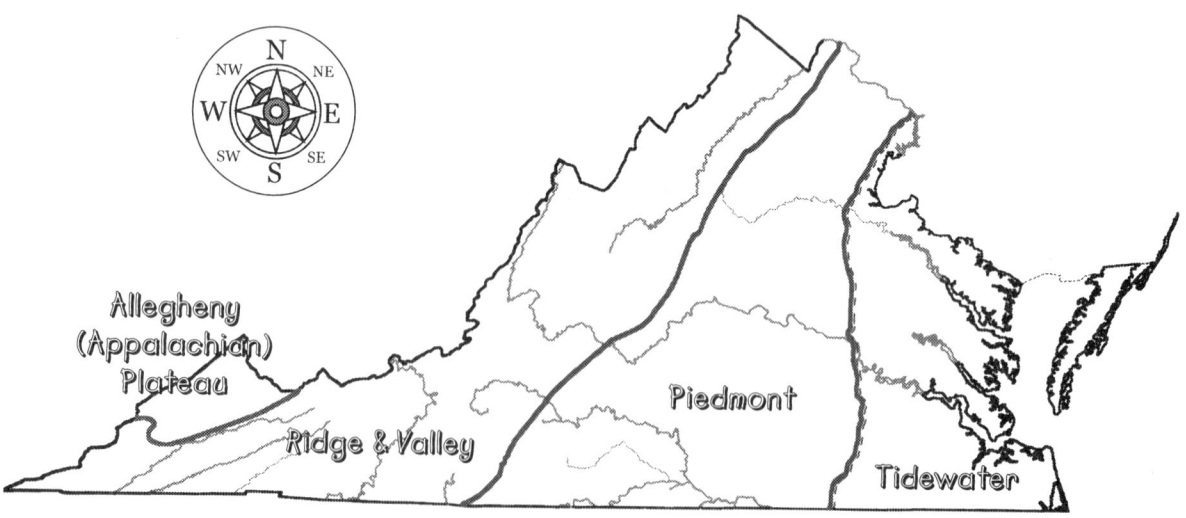

Here Come the Europeans!

Europeans: people who live in or come from the continent of Europe

Europeans who came to Virginia settled in different parts of the state.

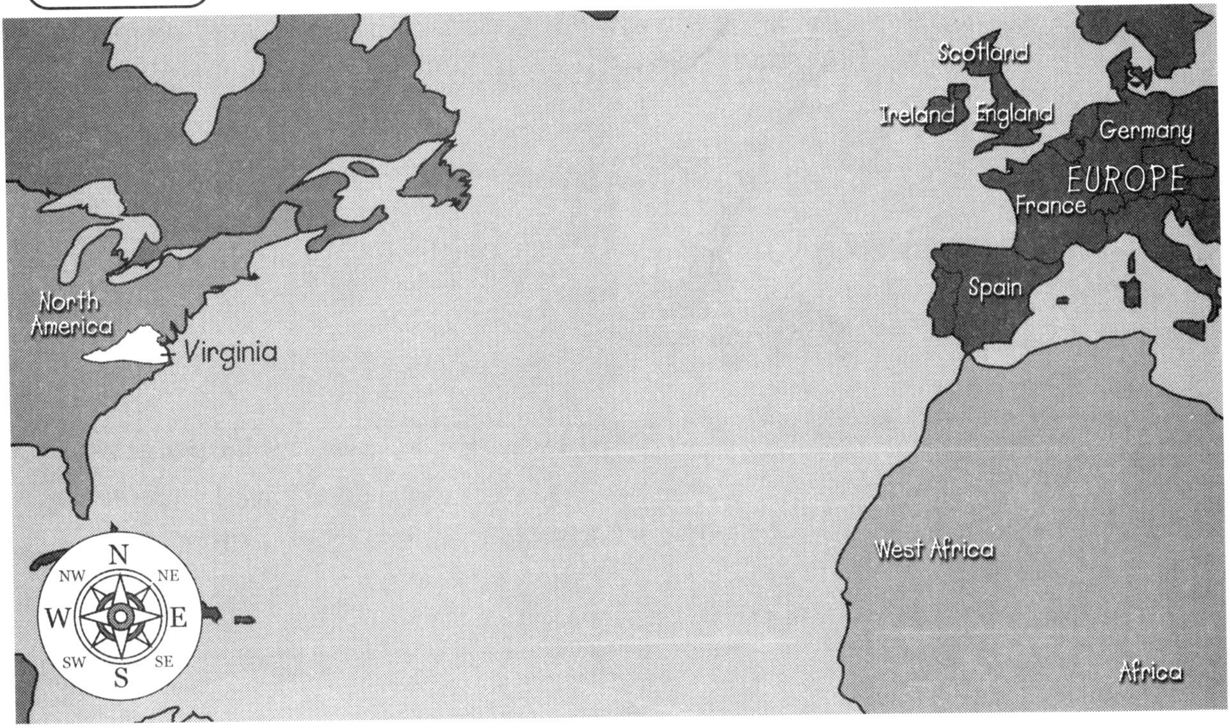

Draw a dashed (— — —) line from the coast of England to the coast of Virginia.

The English settled in Jamestown at the mouth of the James River for three very good reasons:
- The area was rich in natural resources.
- The river had a good harbor.
- The location was easy to defend.

English: people who live in or come from the country of England

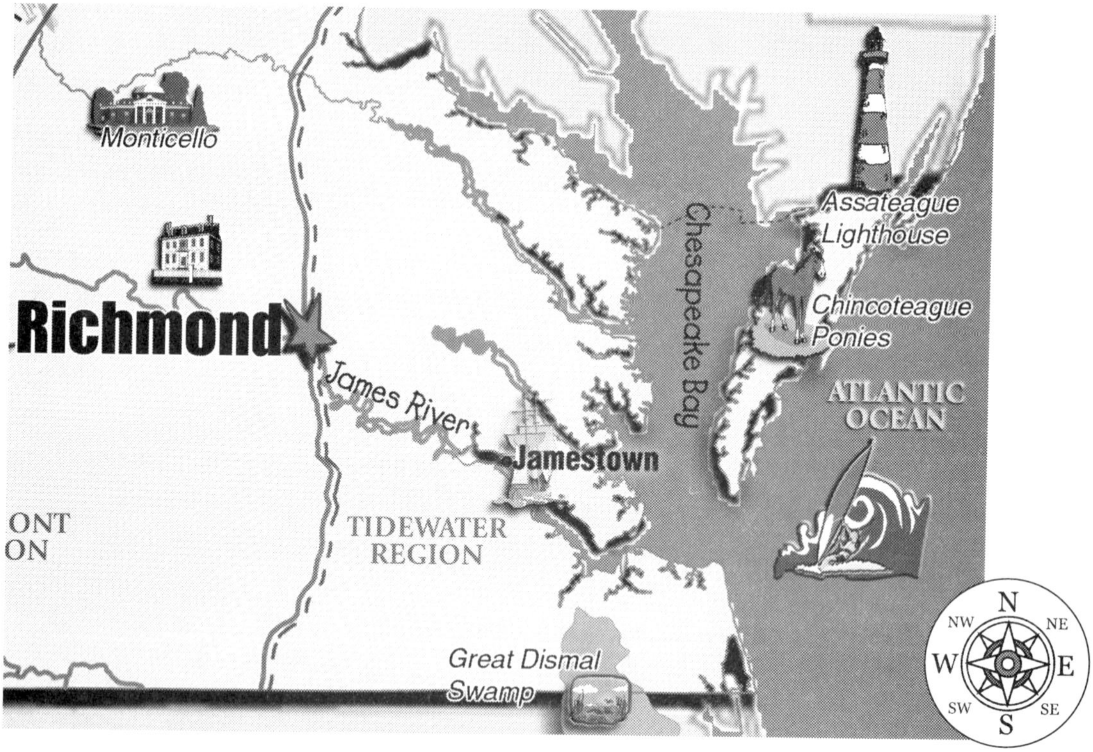

 **Put a ● on the area where the English settled when they first came to Virginia.**

The Scottish, Irish, and Germans settled in the Shenandoah Valley of Virginia. They settled here because of the rich farm land.

 **Match the people on the left with the country they came from on the right.**

Scottish   Ireland
Irish   Germany
German   Scotland

Circle the names of the countries that sent settlers to Virginia.

Fertile farm land was important to the early settlers because they needed to grow crops in order to feed themselves.

On the map below draw symbols from the map key to show the crops the early settlers grew.

MAP KEY
- Tobacco
- Beans
- Corn
- Apples
- Squash

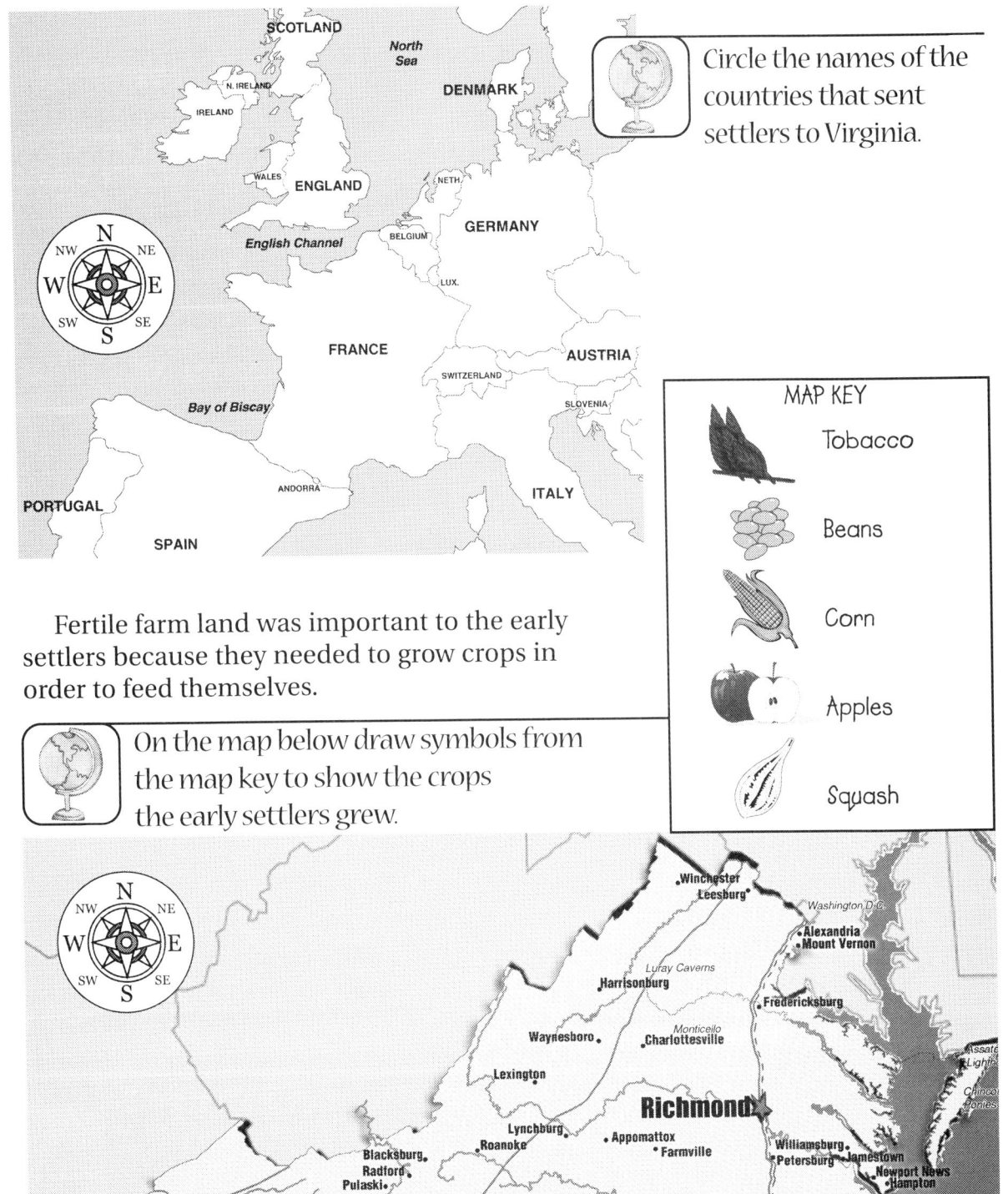

African Slaves Come to Virginia

African slaves were brought to Virginia as a source of labor. As plantations in the Tidewater region expanded, more hands were needed to work the land. People were brought by ship from Africa to work for free. They were needed to plant, grow, and harvest the crops.

slave: a person who is owned by another person

 Draw a dashed (– – – –) line from Africa to Virginia.

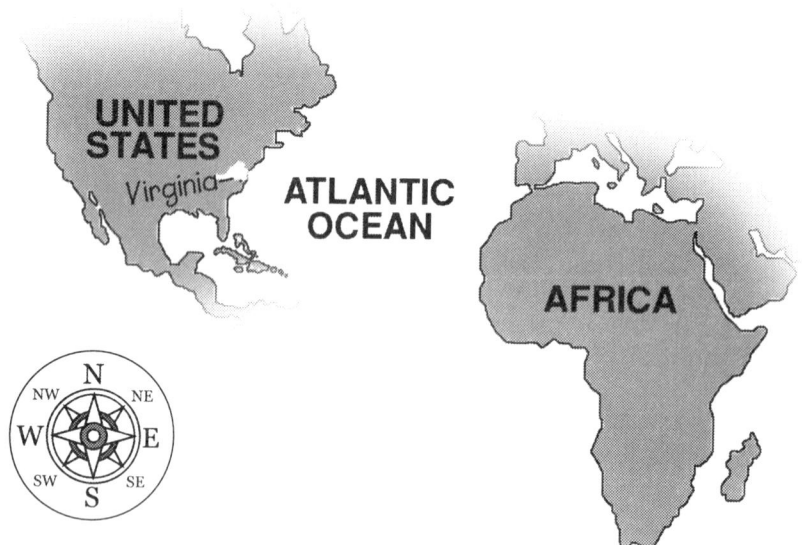

Circle the region in Virginia where African slaves were first brought to work.

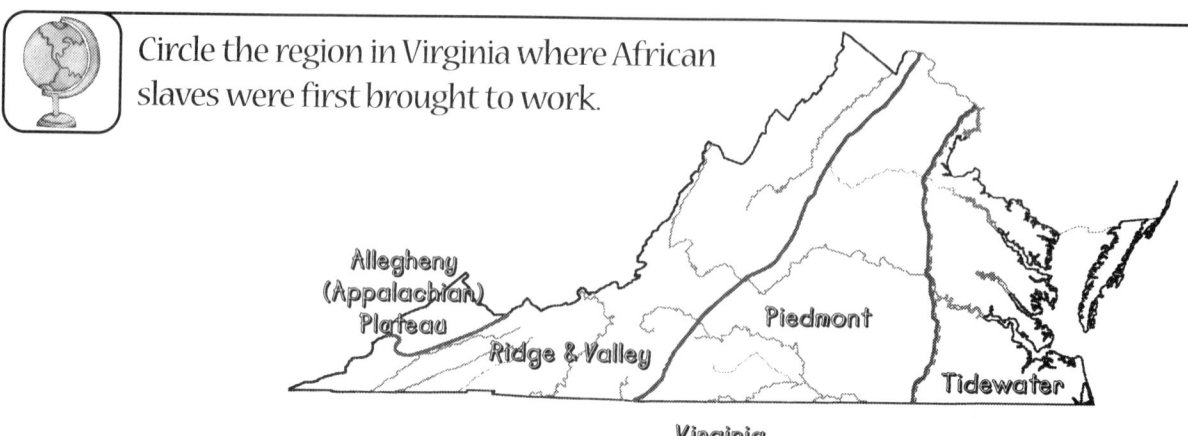

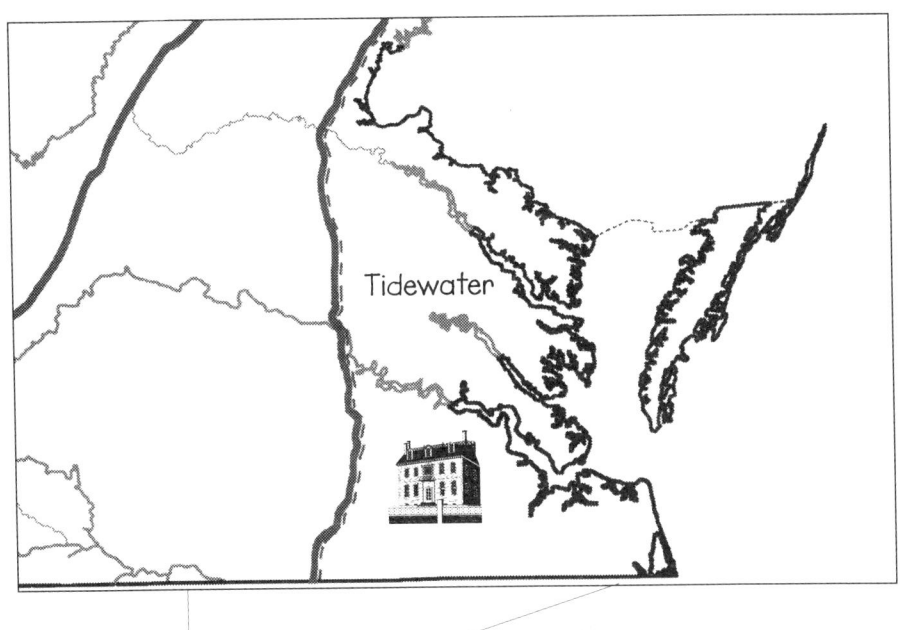
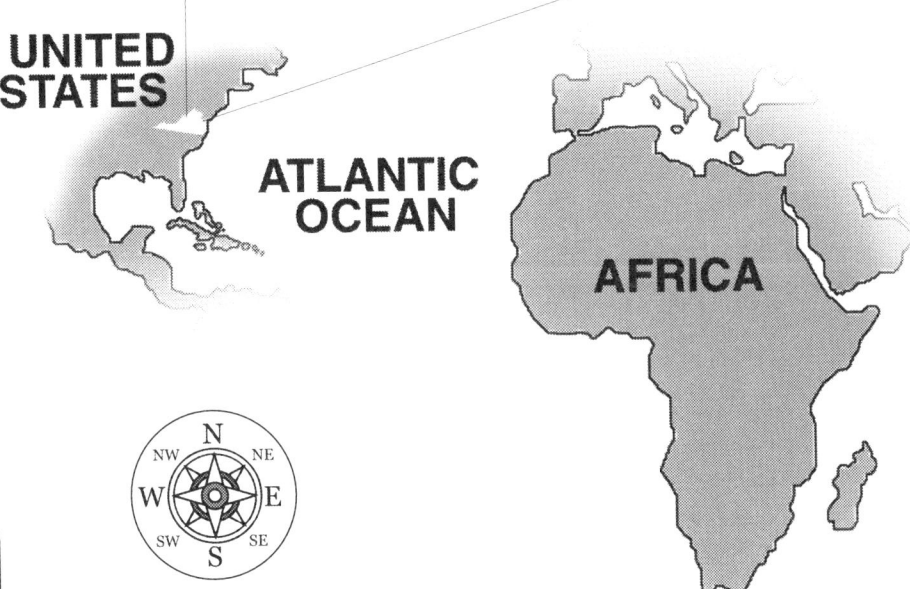

Locate Africa on the map. ....Write an "S" for Slaves.
Locate the Tidewater region of Virginia. ....Write an "L" for labor.
Locate the Atlantic Ocean. ....Write an "A" on the Atlantic Ocean.
Locate Virginia on the map. ....Write a "V" for Virginia.
Locate a plantation in the Tidewater region. ......Write an "E" for expansion.

Why Move?

Settlers who first came to Virginia settled along the coast. Soon, they began to move inland to other parts of the state.

What causes people to move from one location to another? Here are just a few reasons:

Necessity: They may need more space to grow crops.

Preference: Perhaps they prefer a cooler climate, a city over the countryside, or to be closer to their work, other family members, or new opportunities.

Curiosity: Some people want to try new places, to see different areas.

Opportunity: They may even believe that there are better opportunities in other geographic locations than where they currently live and work.

How many times have you moved so far in your lifetime? ☐

How many states have you lived in? ☐
Name them:

_____

_____

How many towns/cities have you lived in? ☐
Name them:

_____

_____

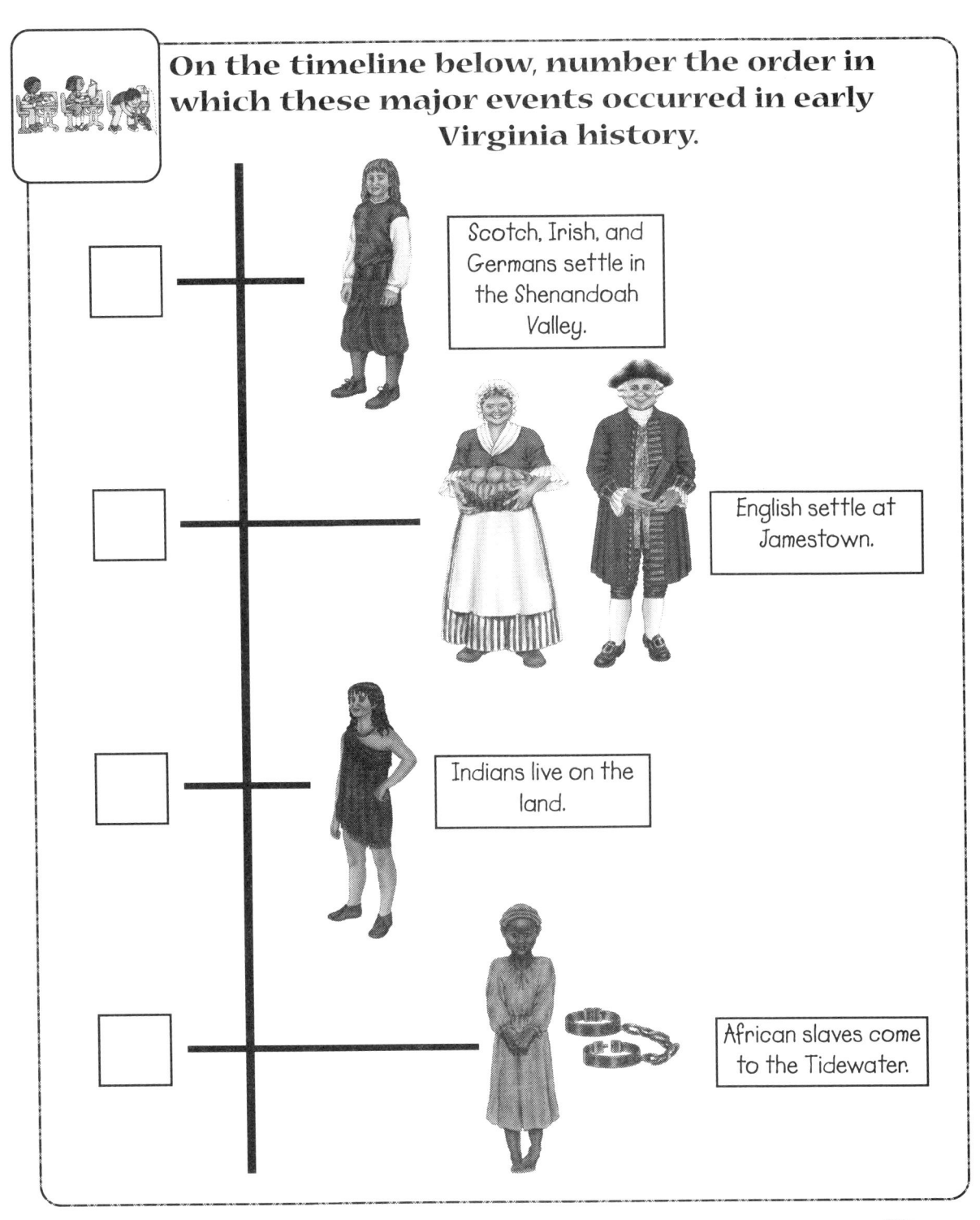

On the timeline below, number the order in which these major events occurred in early Virginia history.

- Scotch, Irish, and Germans settle in the Shenandoah Valley.
- English settle at Jamestown.
- Indians live on the land.
- African slaves come to the Tidewater.

A Quick Review for YOU!

1. The first people who lived in Virginia were _____ _____.

2. The _____ Indians were part of the Algonquian language group.

3. Indians who lived in the Piedmont region were part of the _____ language group.

4. Indians who spoke the Iroquian language lived in the Allegheny (Appalachian) _____.

5. The English settled at the mouth of the _____ River.

6. The Scottish, Irish, and Germans settled in the _____ Valley.

7. African _____ worked for free on Tidewater plantations.

One More - Just For Fun!

You are about to become the first settler in a New World! You can only take six items with you. List the things you will take.

_____   _____

_____   _____

_____   _____

4.1b - The geographic features of Virginia affected the location and growth of its cities.

The Development of Virginia's Cities

As Virginia grew, cities developed along the Atlantic Ocean, the Chesapeake Bay, and the state's major rivers. Geographic factors affected where cities were located and how they grew.

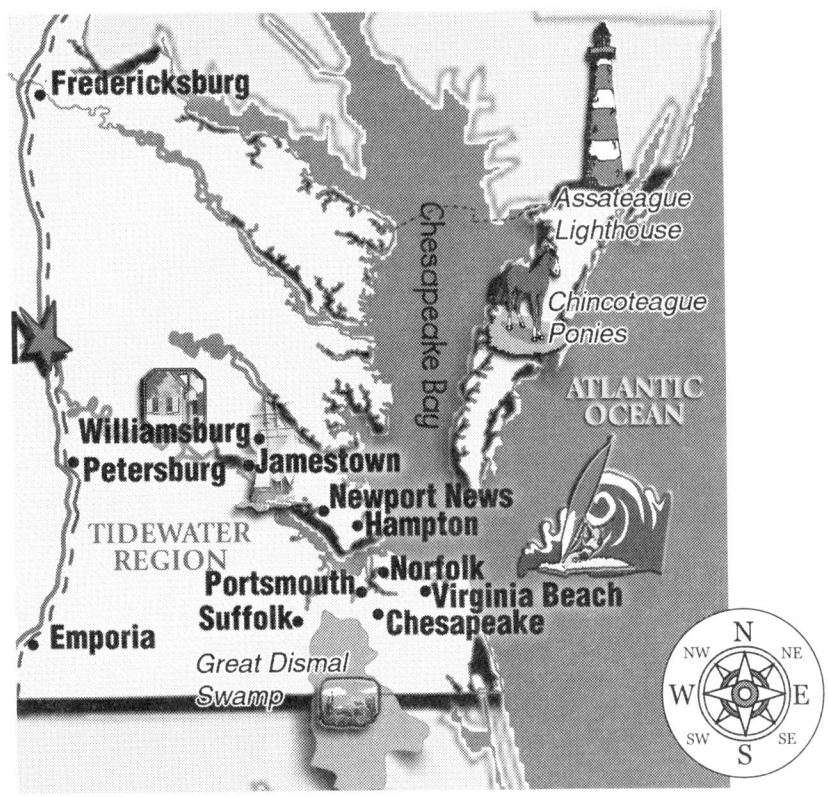

• Cities developed in areas that had access to the Atlantic Ocean.

 Circle three cities that have access to the Atlantic Ocean.

 **Circle the reasons a city might develop along the ocean:**

shipping   coal mining   fishing   farming

- Cities developed around the mouth of the Chesapeake Bay because of its rich natural resources and its natural harbor. These cities included Norfolk, Hampton, and Yorktown.

harbor: a part of a body of water deep enough to anchor a ship

natural resources: things that exist in or are formed by nature

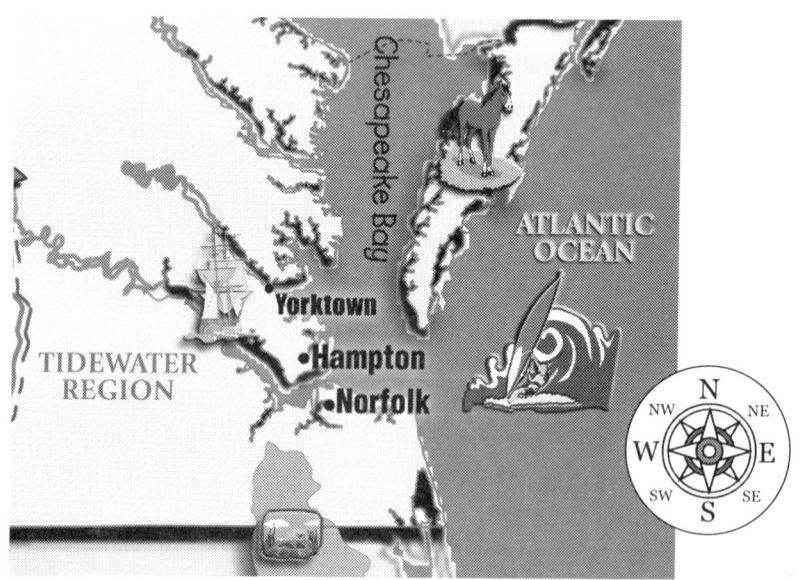

 Write the name of the body of water that the three cities shown grew up around:

_____

fall line: boundary between an upland region and a coastal plain

• Cities developed along the fall line because it formed a natural barrier to river transportation. One example is the city of Richmond on the James River.

 Trace the dashed line that some Virginia cities grew up alongside.

1. This line is called the _____ line.

2. Circle four cities that developed along the fall line.

• Cities developed along rivers, because rivers were the main transportation routes in early Virginia. One example is Alexandria on the Potomac River.

 **3.** Write the name of a city that developed along the Potomac River: _____

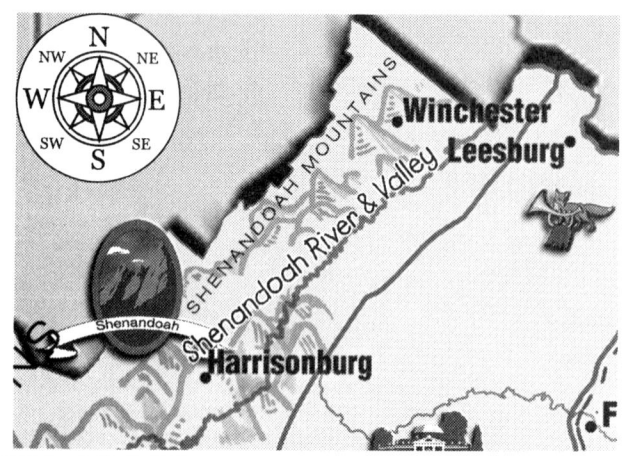

• Cities developed in the Shenandoah Valley because of its rich soil and the natural shelter of the mountains. Two examples of such cities are Harrisonburg and Winchester.

The cities of Winchester and Harrisonburg developed in the Shenandoah Valley because of:

    A. nearness to the Atlantic Ocean
    B. being close to the mouth of a river
    C. rich soil and mountain shelter

A Quick Review for YOU!

1. Virginia cities grew up along the _____ Ocean and the _____ Bay.

2. The natural barrier to river transportation in Virginia is called the _____ _____.

3. The main transportation routes in early Virginia were its _____.

4. Cities that developed in the natural shelter of the mountains were in the area called the _____ Valley.

Chapter 2

Nine of the ten largest cities in Virginia can be found on the Eastern Seaboard or along the Fall Line. Virginia Beach is the largest city in Virginia and one of the fastest-growing cities in the United States. Its population increased by 50 percent between 1980 and 1990.

4.2a - Map tools and skills help us find our way around Virginia and the world!

Map Tools Help Us Find Our Way Around!

One very useful map tool is the directional indicator called a *compass rose*. A compass rose helps us identify and use *cardinal directions*. The cardinal directions are: north, south, east, and west. Some map direction indicators also include *intermediate directions*: northeast, northwest, southeast, and southwest. A simple map might only show a *north pointer*, an arrow indicating which direction is due north.

COMPASS ROSE

Another useful map tool is a map *key*, also called a map *legend*. This shows symbols which represent different things on a map.

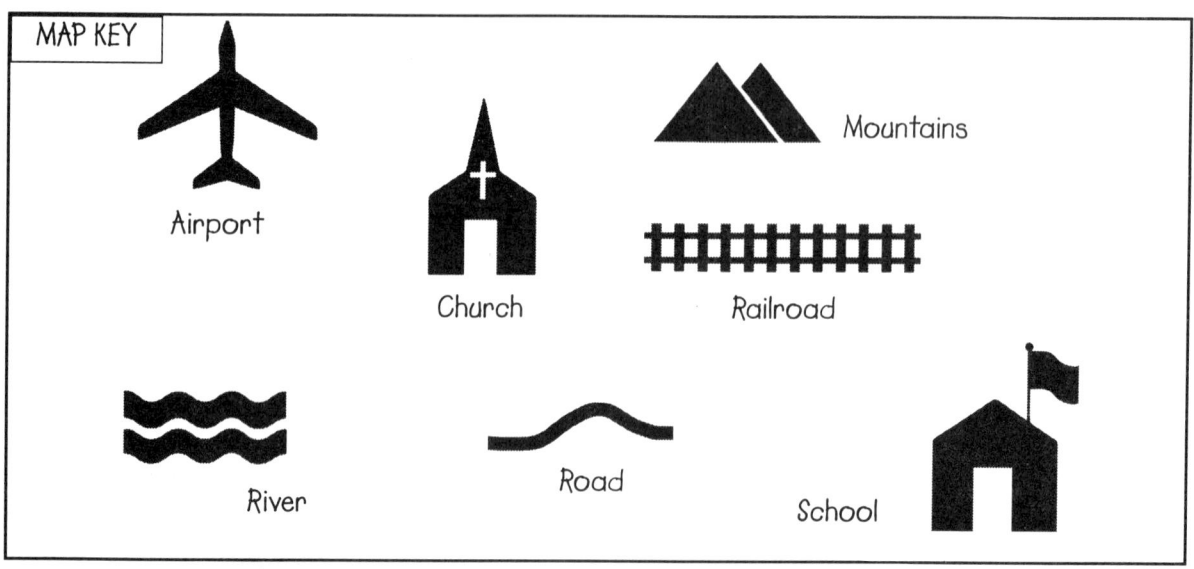

Where Are We Located?

The absolute location of a place can be described by using a grid system. A location grid on a map usually consists of letters and numbers identifying a network of lines up and down and back and forth across the map. Here is an example of a grid system.

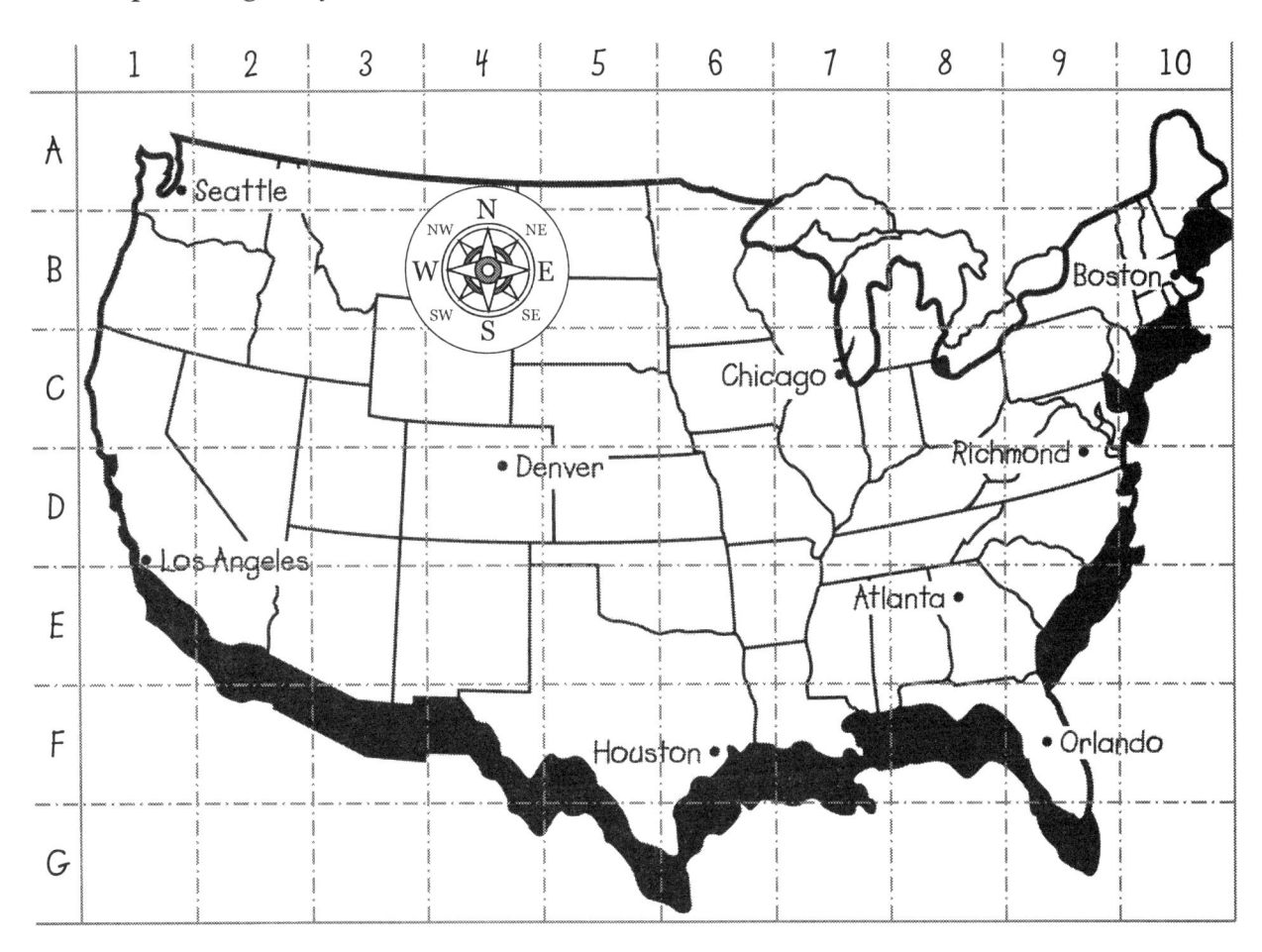

The grid columns (vertical sections) are numbered from 1 to 10. The grid rows (horizontal sections) are lettered from A to G.

Looking at this map, Seattle is in A-1, Los Angeles in D-1, Denver in D-4, Houston in F-6, Chicago in C-7, Atlanta in E-8, Orlando in F-9 and Boston in B-10.

Virginia's capital, Richmond, is in: _____ - _____
                                                 letter   number

Grids help us find places on maps, and grids may change from map to map. For example, on the previous map, Richmond was in grid block D-9. We can find the location of Virginia's capital city of Richmond on the map below by using the letter and number codes of the map's grid.

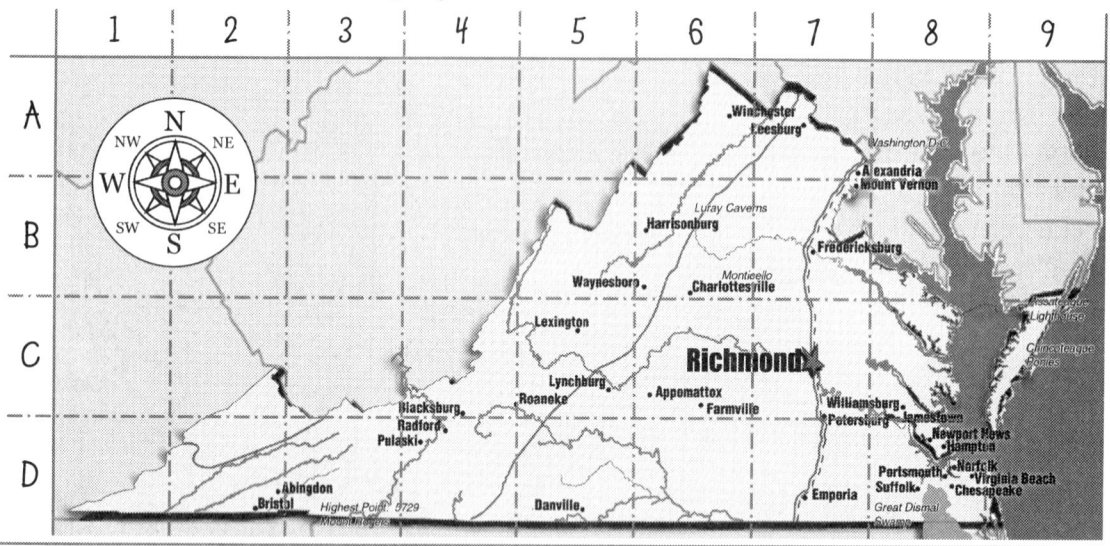

Richmond is located at this letter: _____ and this number: _____.

The *geographic location* of Richmond can be described by using *longitude* and *latitude*. Geographers did us a favor by creating imaginary lines that run around the globe to help us locate our position. These lines are:

longitude: which run vertically north and south around the globe

latitude: which run horizontally east and west around the globe (Lines of latitude are also called *parallels*.)

Positions are measured in Degrees(°)

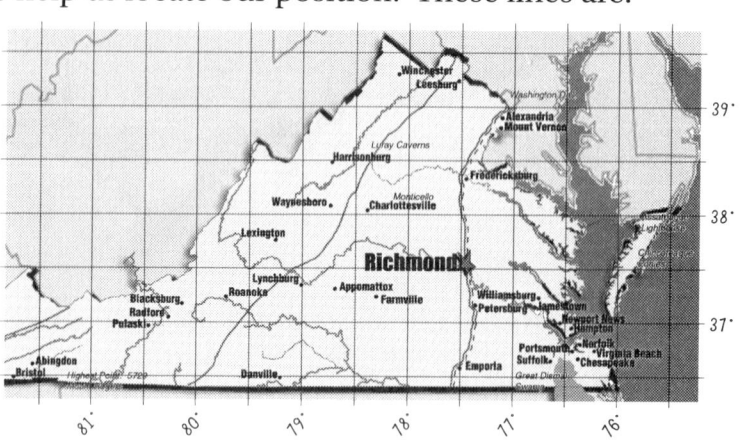

Richmond is located between
37° and 38° N latitude by 77° and 78° W longitude.

More Map Skills!

We use a map to find the *relative location* of a place. You can determine where a place is by looking to see what other places it is near. For example, Virginia's eastern border is formed by the Potomac River and the Atlantic Ocean. Virginia also borders these states: Maryland, West Virginia, Kentucky, Tennessee, and North Carolina.

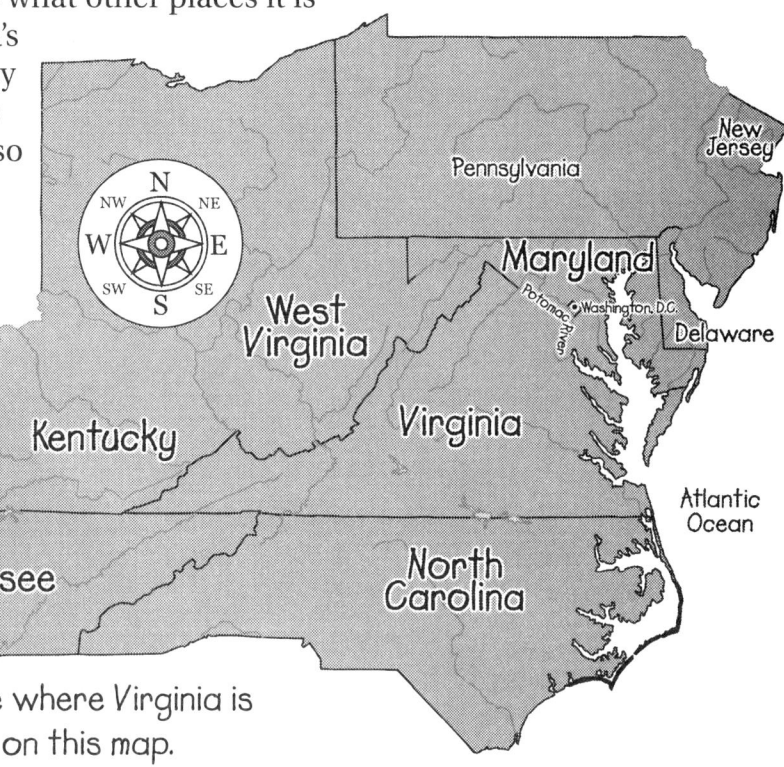

It is easy to see where Virginia is located on this map.

 **Use the compass rose to answer these questions:**

1. Virginia is bordered on the south by the states of: _____ and _____ _____.

2. _____ and _____ _____ are the states west of Virginia.

3. The _____ _____ forms Virginia's northeastern border.

4. The ocean bordering Virginia is the _____ _____.

On this map, can you find the state of Virginia, just by looking at some of the places it is near?

If so, write its name on the state.

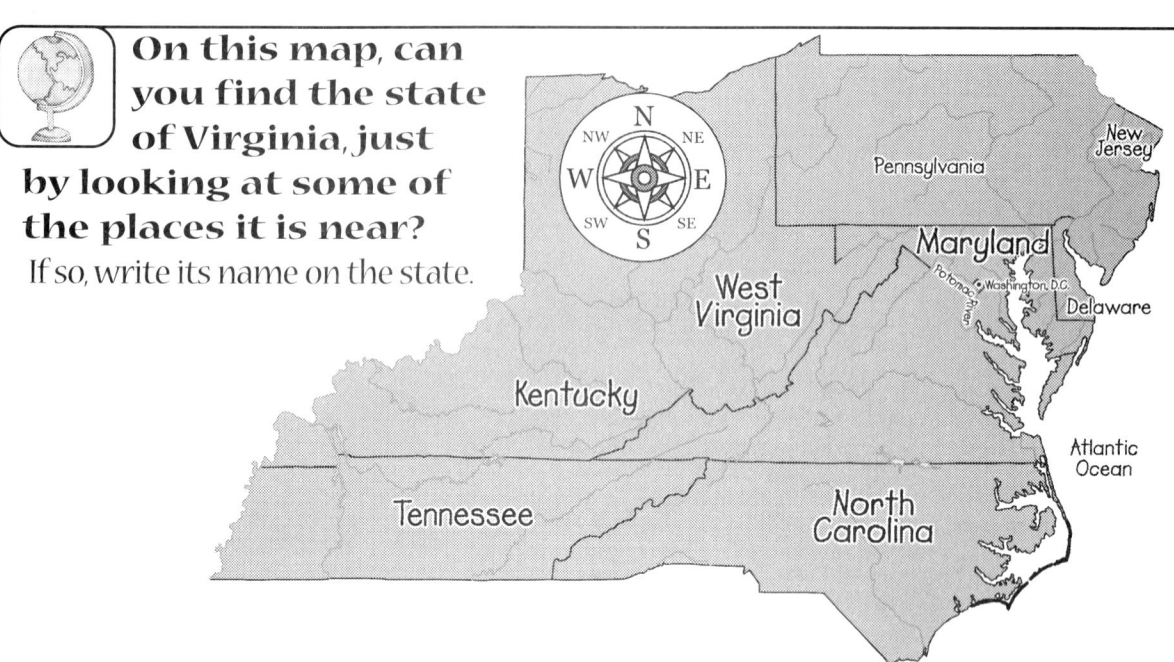

Virginia is one of the 50 United States. Here is a map of the United States.

Label the state of Virginia with its postal abbreviation, VA.

~ This book is not reproducible. ~

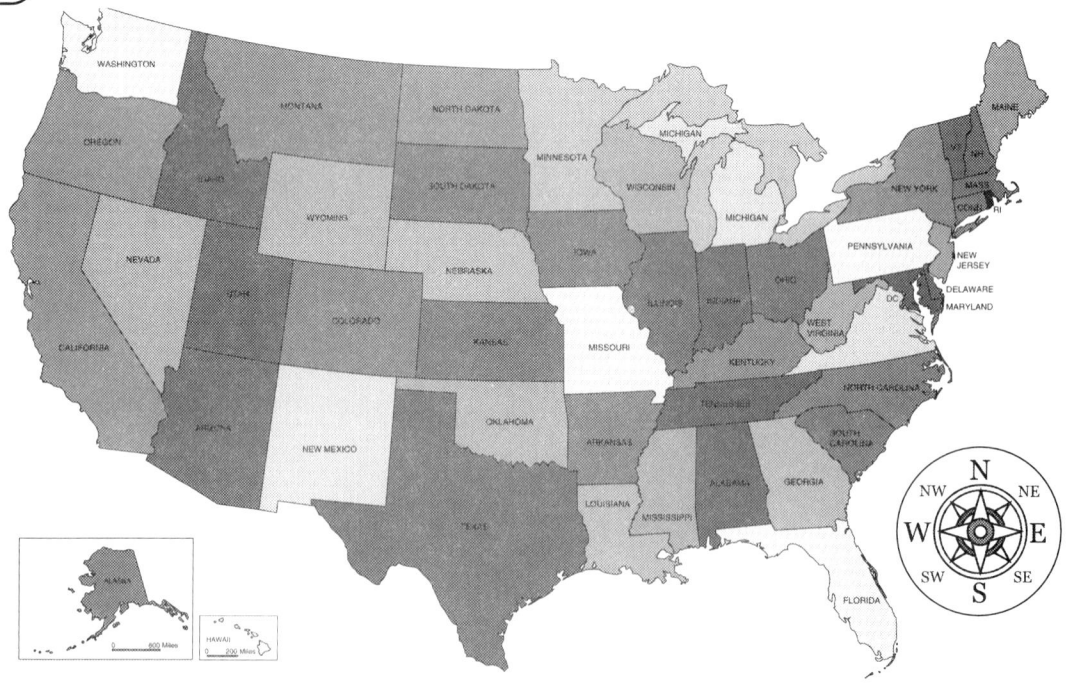

Virginia was one of the thirteen original states.

Look at the states on this map.

Label Virginia on the map.

The original colonists came to Virginia and the other colonies from Western Europe.

On the map below, draw a solid line on the route that colonists may have taken from Western Europe to the state of Virginia.

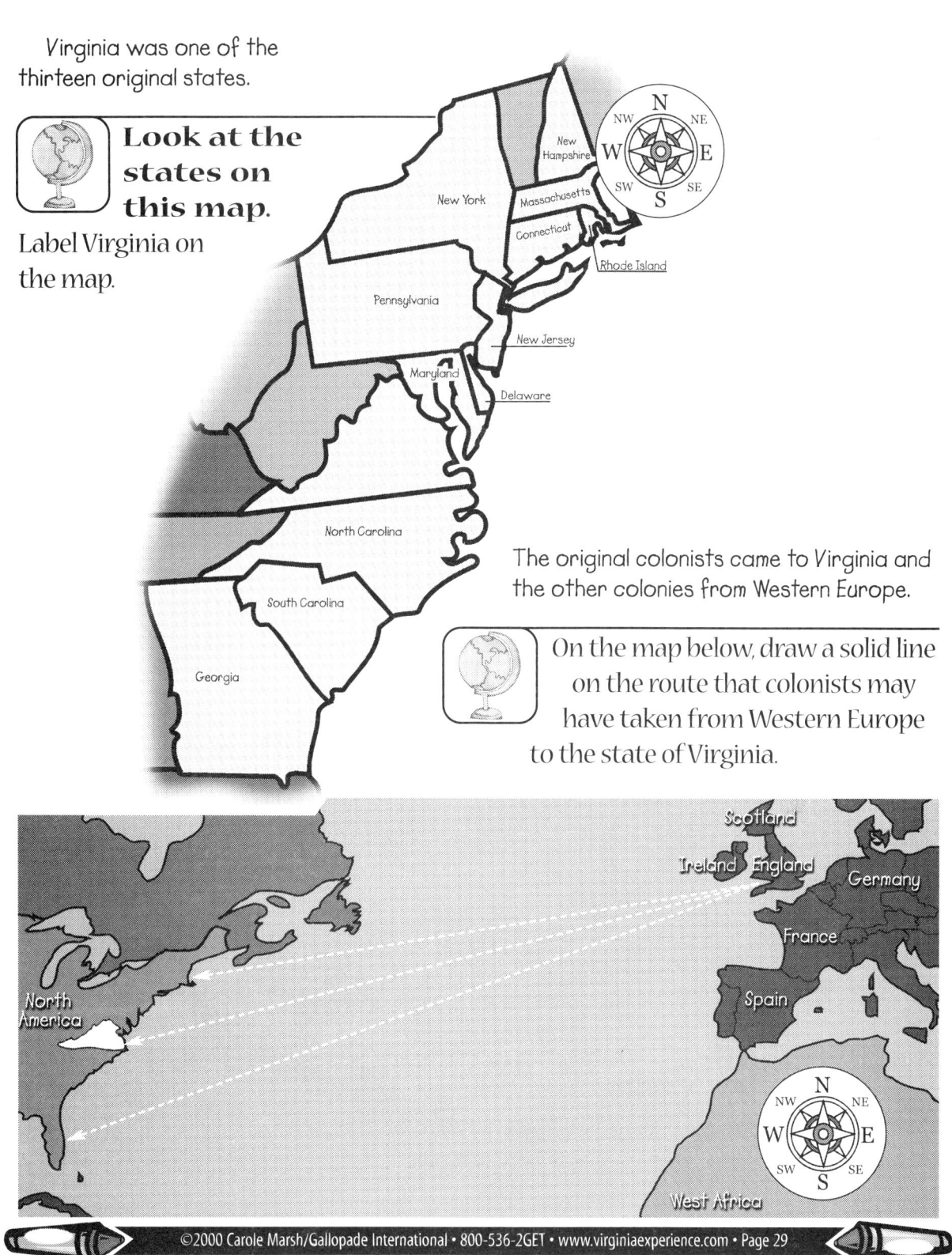

Slaves sailed over the Atlantic Ocean to Virginia and other colonies from West Africa.

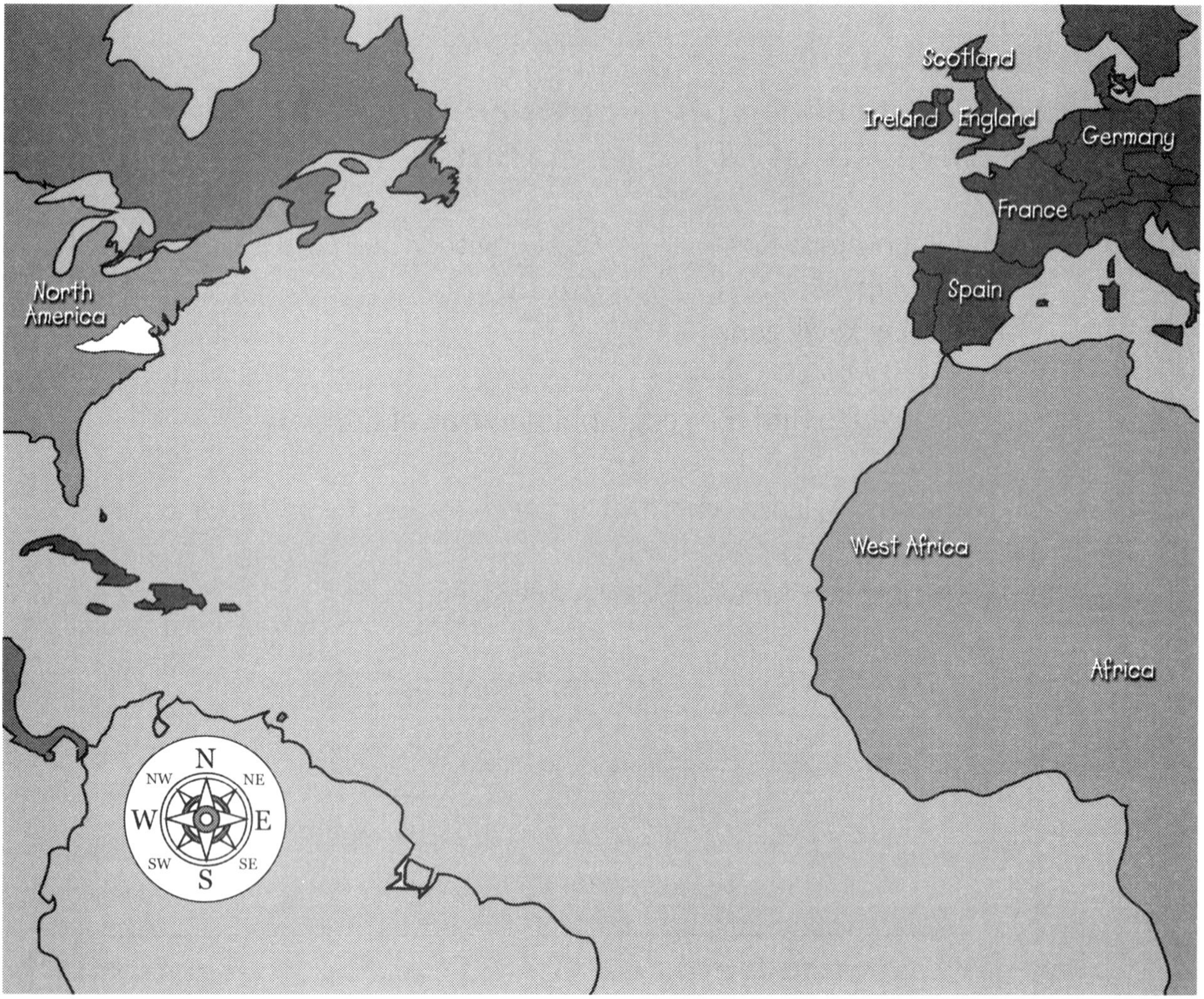

 Draw a straight line (————) showing a possible route from West Africa to Virginia.

Draw a dashed line (- - - -) showing a possible route from England to Virginia.

Over what body of water were slaves transported to Virginia? Write the ocean's name on the center of the map.

Here is a list of handy geographic tools.

Beside each item you need to accomplish, put the initials of the tool that can best help you!

(CR) Compass Rose (LL) Longitude and Latitude
(M) Map   (G) Grid
(K) Map key/legend

1. _____ I need to find the geographic location of Germany.

2. _____ I need to learn where an airport is located near Norfolk.

3. _____ I need to find which way is north.

4. _____ I need to chart a route from Virginia to California.

5. _____ I need to find a small town on a map.

Match the items on the left with the items on the right.

1. Grid system
2. Compass rose
3. Longitude and latitude
4. Two of Virginia's borders
5. Symbols on a map

A. Map key or legend
B. West Virginia and the Atlantic Ocean
C. A system of letters and numbers
D. Imaginary lines around the earth
E. Shows N, S, E, and W

Home, Sweet Home!
Put an X where your home city, town, or county is located in Virginia.

The name of my city/town is: _____

The name of my county is: _____

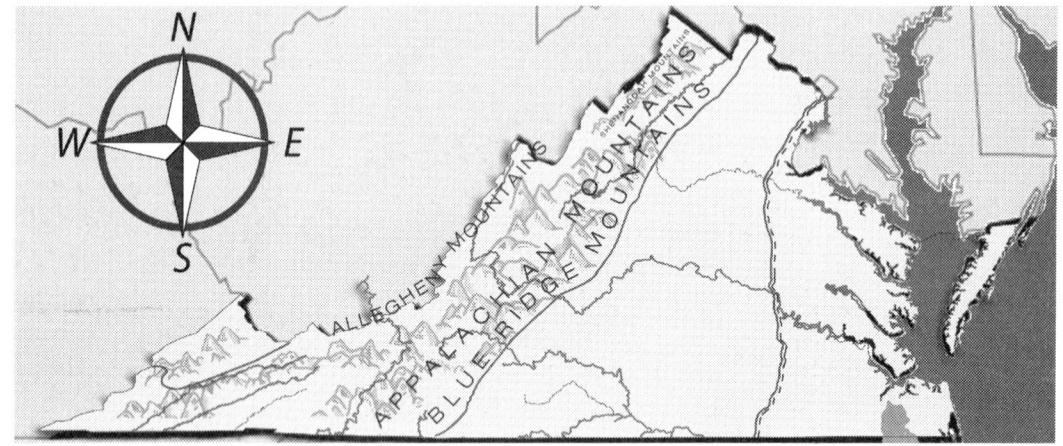

Geography Careers!
You love geography? I'm so glad! Perhaps you'd like to consider a career as one of the following:

anthropogeographer: studies people and geography
cartographer: mapmaker
climatologist: studies the weather
economic geographer: studies resources of an area and finds locations for industries
geographer: studies the physical earth
geologist: examines rocks for earth's history
mathematical geographer: studies parallels and meridians
meteorologist: weather forecaster
oceanographer: studies waves, tides, and currents
physiographer: studies land forms
political geographer: plans government boundaries

This type of geography interests me most: _____

4.2b - Physical characteristics, transportation routes, climate, and specialization influenced the variety of crops, products, and industries, and the general patterns of economic growth in Virginia.

Let's Get Physical!

natural resources: present in or produced by nature

Physical characteristics influence how people live in a region. Physical characteristics can include the type of soil, available water, and natural resources. Other things that can affect how Virginians live include climate, transportation routes, and specialization. All of these things can influence the products, industries, and economic growth of a region. Let's see how!

Virginia's waterways and natural harbors encouraged the development of:

- shipbuilding in Portsmouth
- shipping in Norfolk
- fishing in the Chesapeake Bay
- tourism in the Tidewater region

Use the information above to answer these questions:

1. A major body of water for fishing: _____

2. A major deep water port for shipping: _____

3. A major shipbuilding center: _____

4. A place tourists enjoy: _____

The abundant forests and fertile soil of Virginia encouraged the development of lumbering and farming in the Piedmont and in the Ridge and Valley region.

Circle the correct choices...

1. Lumbering requires:
   A. tourism offices
   B. abundant forests
   C. no rain

2. A successful farm requires:
   A. coal fields
   B. waterways
   C. fertile soil

The temperate climate in Virginia allowed for the growth of tobacco in the Tidewater region, corn in the Piedmont region, and apples in the Ridge and Valley region.

The rich mineral deposits allowed for growth in the mining of coal in the Allegheny (Appalachian) Plateau.

temperate: mild; neither too hot, nor too cold

Match the map key symbols with the region in Virginia where you are most likely to find this resource, crop, or product.

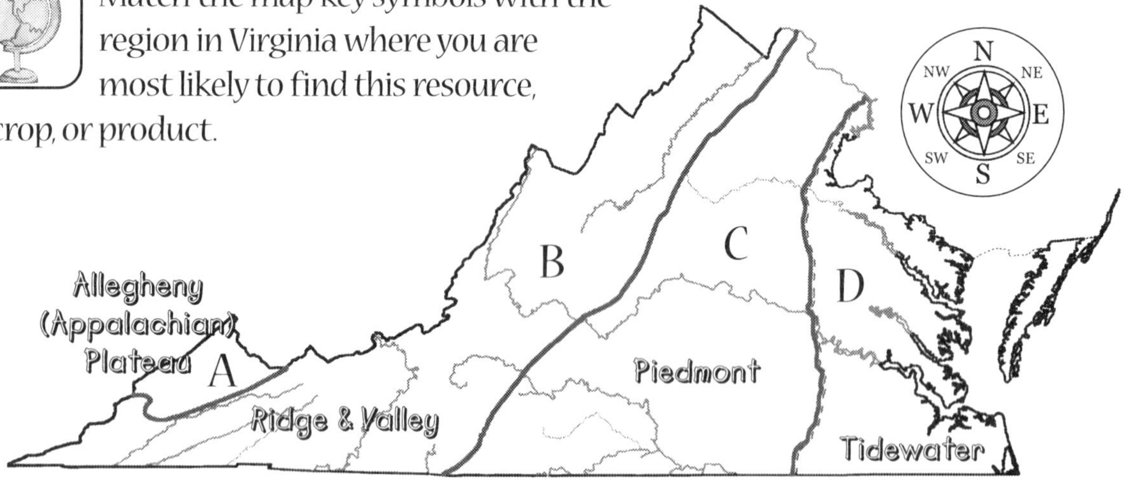

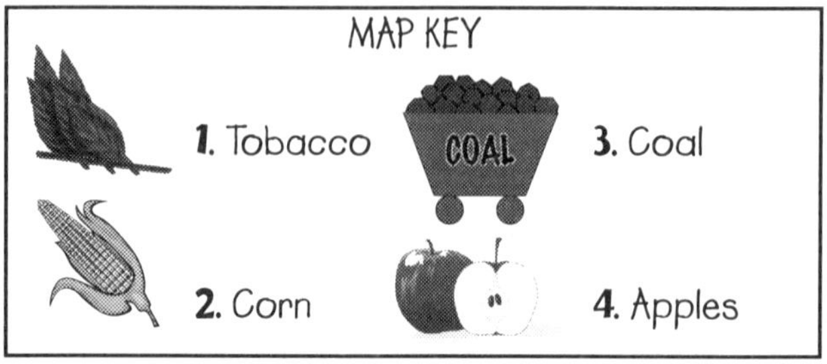

MAP KEY
1. Tobacco
2. Corn
3. Coal
4. Apples

Answers:
A ☐ B ☐
C ☐ D ☐

Virginia on the Go!

Transportation routes influenced economic growth in Virginia. Railroads and interstate highways provide a way to get goods to markets and raw materials to manufacturing centers.

A. You have just harvested your crop of apples. They need to get to market quickly before they spoil. Write an **A** in the box next to the transportation method that you could best use to achieve this goal.

B. You have mined twenty tons of coal. It is time to get it to a processing plant on the coast. Write a **B** in the box next to the transportation method that will allow you to do this most effectively.

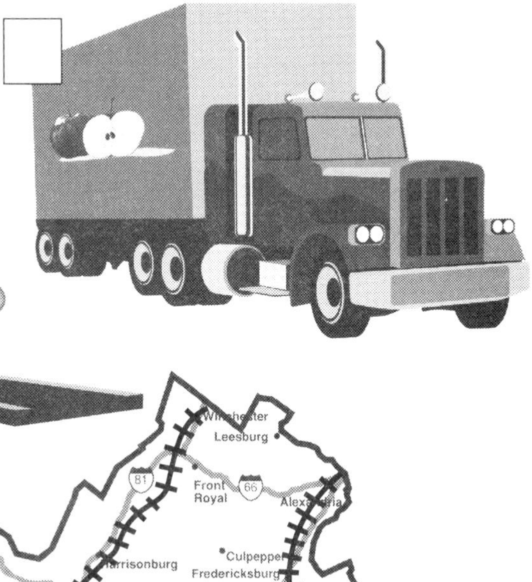

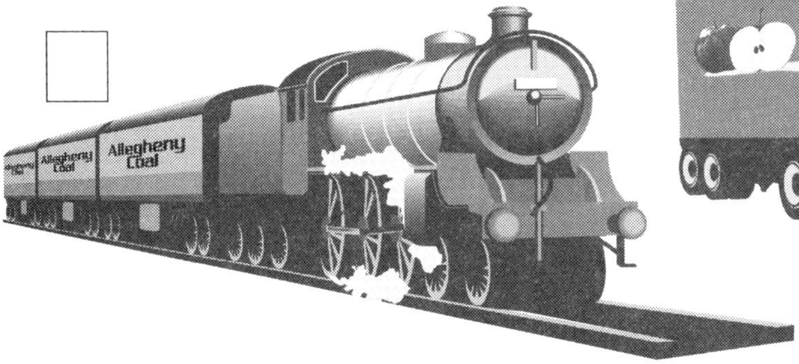

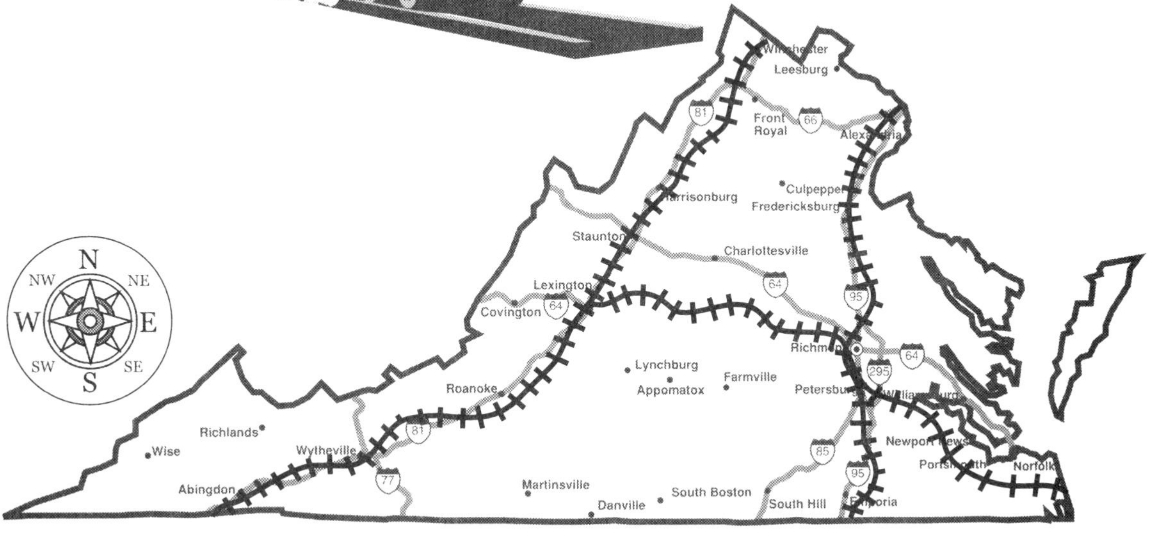

We Are Special!

Different areas of Virginia are noted for specializing in certain things. This specialization helped these areas to grow economically. For example:
- Federal government offices and high technology industries are located in Northern Virginia.
- Textile factories are located in the Danville area.

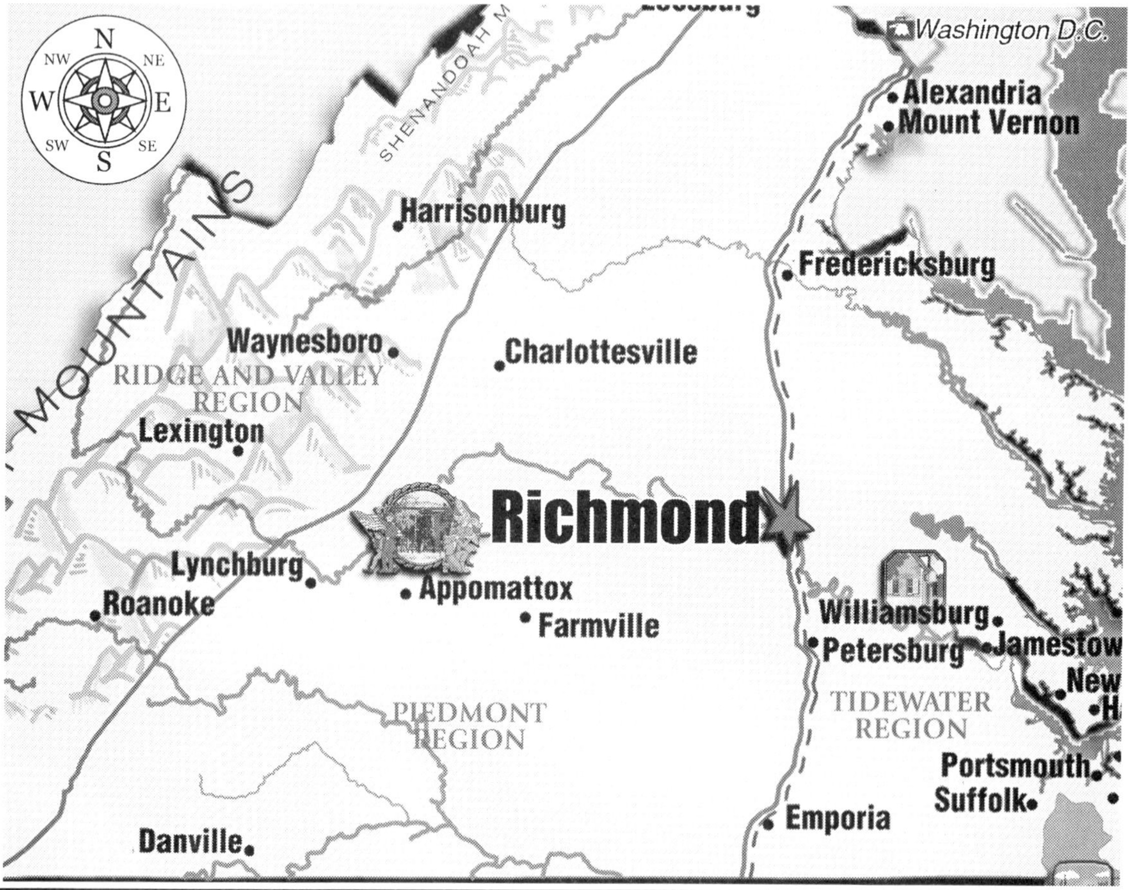

 Draw the symbols from the map key on the Virginia location where they most apply.

Weather Report!

Match the weather forecast with the person it will hurt most!

A. hurricane! 1. farmers
B. no rain 2. fishermen

Match the weather forecast with the person it will help most!

A. sunny and warm 1. farmers
B. gentle rain 2. tour guide

A Quick Review for YOU!

1. Virginia's waterways and natural _____ encouraged the Tidewater shipping industry.

2. The state's temperate _____ and fertile _____ helped develop the state's farm crops.

3. A natural resource found beneath the Allegheny (Appalachian) Plateau: _____

4. A good way to get goods to market or raw materials to manufacturing centers:
   A. railroads   B. highways
   C. A and B   D. neither A nor B

5. These types of factories are located in and around Danville: _____

6. Looking for a government or high-tech job? There are lots in this part of Virginia:
   A. eastern   B. western
   C. northern   D. southern

One More - Just for Fun!

Tourism is an important Virginia industry. A friend from another state writes and asks you where they should visit in your state and why.

Answer them with enthusiasm!

1. Go to:

2. Reasons:

Hard to Believe But True!

• Visitors can still see evidence of prehistoric giant landslides today in the Jefferson National Forest, near Roanoke. One landslide is more than THREE MILES LONG! Wow!

• Virginia's largest natural lake, Lake Drummond in the Great Dismal Swamp, may have been created by a meteor.

• Prehistoric fossils of snails, shells, corals, and other creatures can be seen in the black limestone squares of the capitol's checkerboard floors. They are estimated to be 400 to 450 million years old!

Virginia X-Files:
 - Lynchburg, 1830s: newspapers reported strange happenings: an earthquake, a hailstorm, a meteor storm, and spooky lights in the sky!
 - Norfolk, 1853: newspapers reported that during a hailstorm, catfish fell from the sky!

4.2c - Virginia's communities differ in physical features, such as land use, population density, architecture, services, and transportation.

Variety is the Spice of Life!

Communities in Virginia differ in many ways. Physical features give different Virginia communities their unique characters. Let's take a look at some areas of Virginia and see how they vary in their physical features.

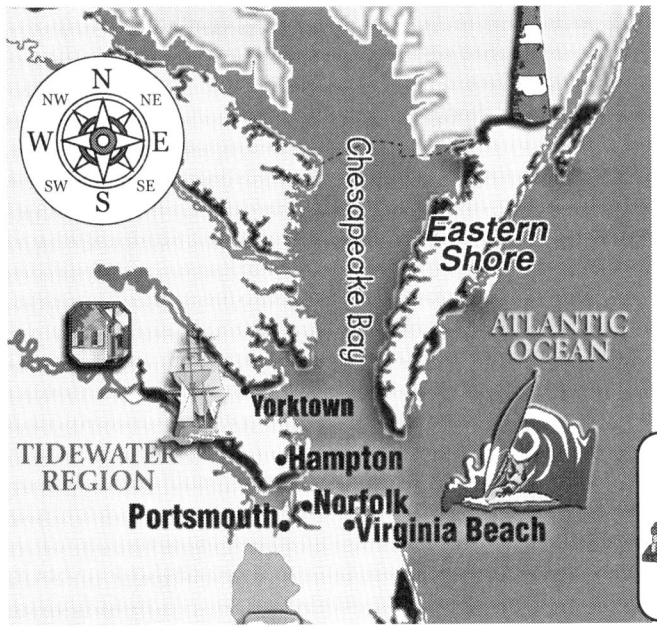

Eastern Shore

Virginia's Eastern Shore is unique because:
- It is located on a peninsula
- Its main industry is fishing
- It has a low population density

peninsula: a body of land surrounded on three sides by water

Circle the land formation that is a peninsula.

(Land is gray, water is white.)

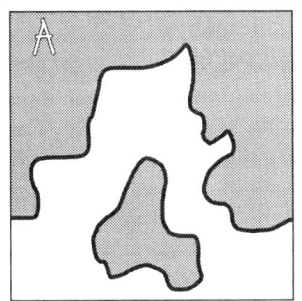

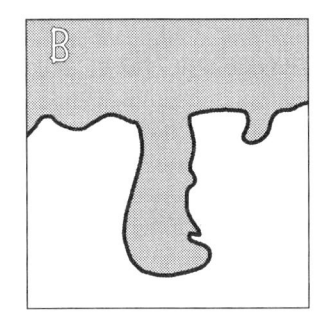

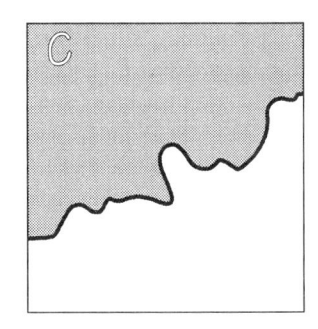

A   B   C

Using the population density map below, answer the following questions:

1. This area has the lowest population density: _____
2. This area probably has a large city located in it: _____
3. This area has an average population density: _____

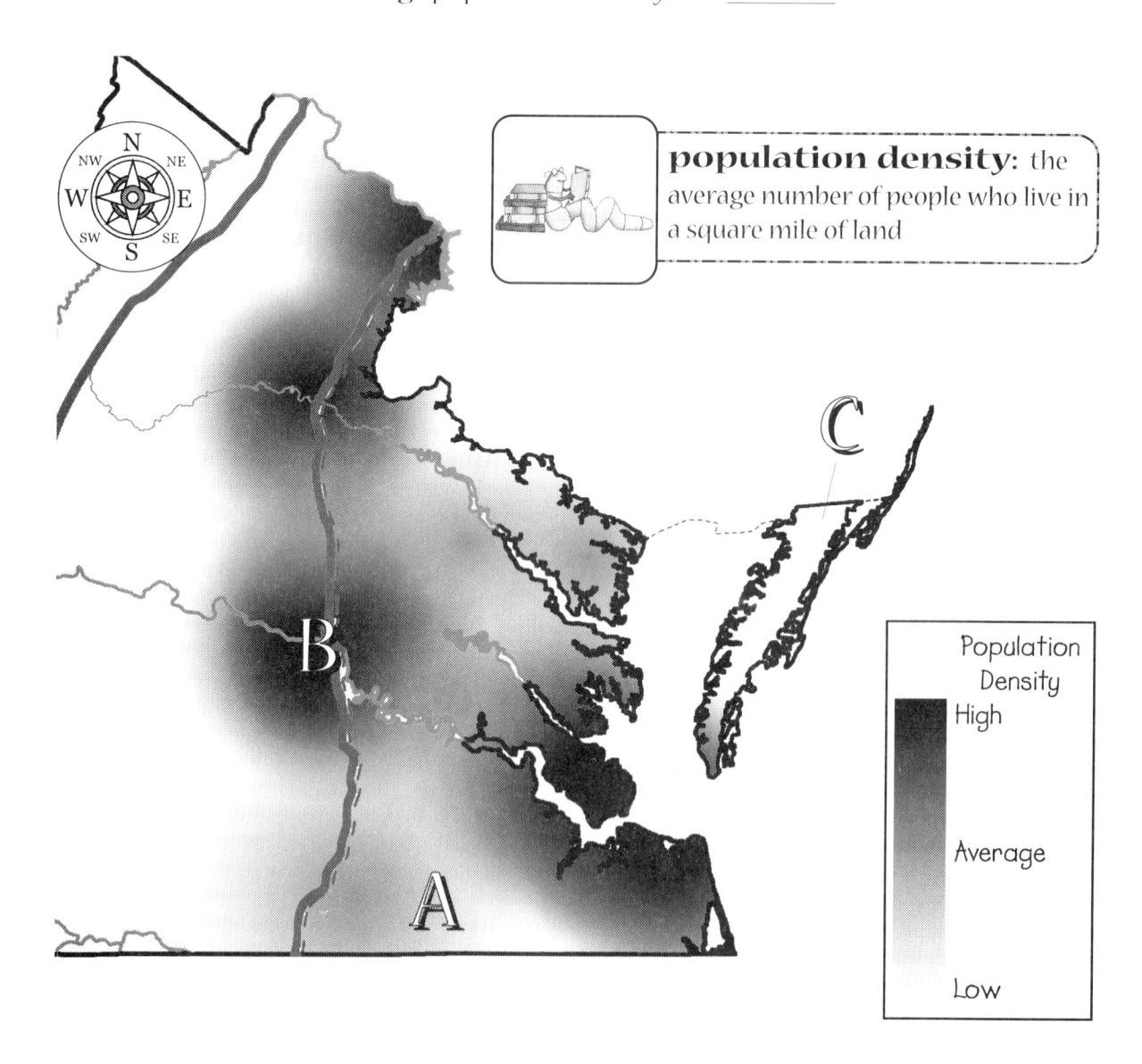

population density: the average number of people who live in a square mile of land

Population Density
High
Average
Low

Take a look at the map of the Eastern Shore.
Which two physical features account for fishing being the area's main industry?

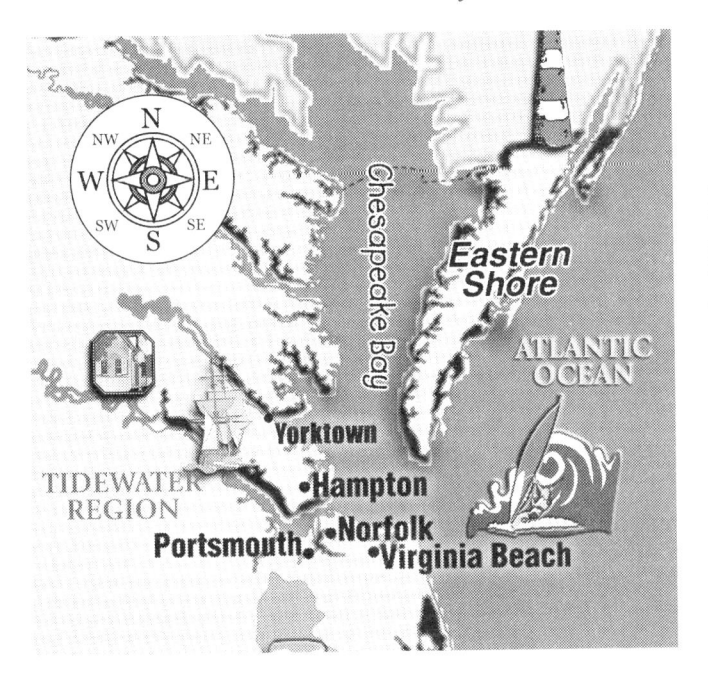

☐ isolation
☐ low population density
☐ abundance of water
☐ being a peninsula

Richmond

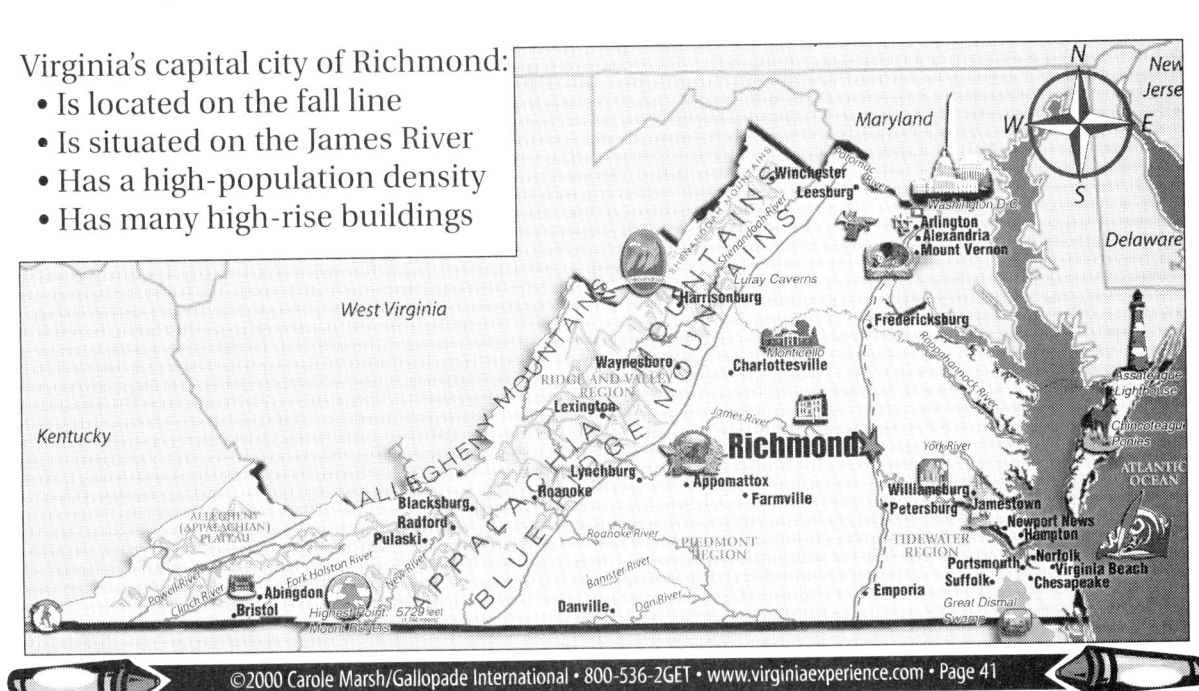

Virginia's capital city of Richmond:
- Is located on the fall line
- Is situated on the James River
- Has a high-population density
- Has many high-rise buildings

The Fall Line

The Tidewater and Piedmont regions of Virginia are separated by a geographic area called a "fall line." This is the place where the rivers fall from a hard rock bed to softer soil and flow toward the Atlantic Ocean. The cities of Alexandria, Fredericksburg, Richmond, Petersburg, and Emporia were settled along this fall line.

Answer the following questions:

1. Richmond has a high population density because:

    A. It is on a fall line
    B. It is on the James River
    C. It has a large number of people living in and around the city

2. The geographic area that separates the Tidewater and Piedmont regions is a:

    A. mountain   B. valley   C. fall line

3. Match the physical characteristics on the left with their appropriate counterpart on the right:

    1. fall line   A. high-rise buildings
    2. high population density   B. cities settled here

4. Which city on the James River was settled on the fall line?

    A. Virginia Beach   B. Richmond   C. Winchester

Northern Virginia

Northern Virginia has a number of physical characteristics which make it different from other communities:

- It is situated near the Potomac River
- It has a high population density
- It has congested highways
- Many U.S. government offices are located here
- It has a rapid transit (Metro) system
- Its architecture includes many high-rise buildings

1. Circle which of the following contributes to the congested highways in Northern Virginia:

2. A good way to avoid congested highways is to: _____

   A. take the rapid transit (Metro) to work
   B. work in a high-rise building
   C. call in sick for work

Shenandoah Valley

The Shenandoah Valley is a beautiful area in western Virginia. Some of its special physical characteristics are:

- It is a valley located between mountains
- The Shenandoah River runs through the valley
- Poultry is one of the main industries in this area
- There are many orchards here
- Numerous caverns are found beneath the earth

valley: a long, narrow piece of low land set between mountains or hills
poultry: chickens, turkeys, ducks, or geese raised for their meat or eggs
orchards: groves of trees which bear fruit
cavern: a large cave or natural opening into or under the earth

Let's Check Out the Shenandoah Valley!

Using the map of the Shenandoah Valley below, answer the following questions:

1. The name of the valley shown between the mountains is the:
   A. Chesapeake   B. Potomac   C. Shenandoah

2. The Shenandoah Valley is the area:
   A. beyond the mountains
   B. between the mountains
   C. beneath the mountains.

3. Write the names of these symbols:
   _____
   _____
   _____

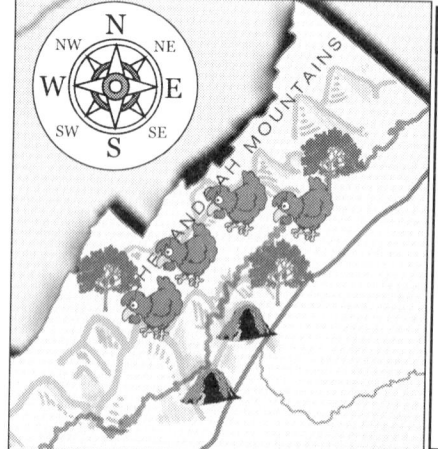

MAP KEY
Caverns
Poultry
Orchards

Southwest Virginia

Southwest Virginia is an area of the state with very different physical characteristics. This area is known for its:

- mountains
- coal mining

Circle the correct answer:

1. You are most likely to find coal mining:

    A. In the mountains
    B. At the shore
    C. In large cities

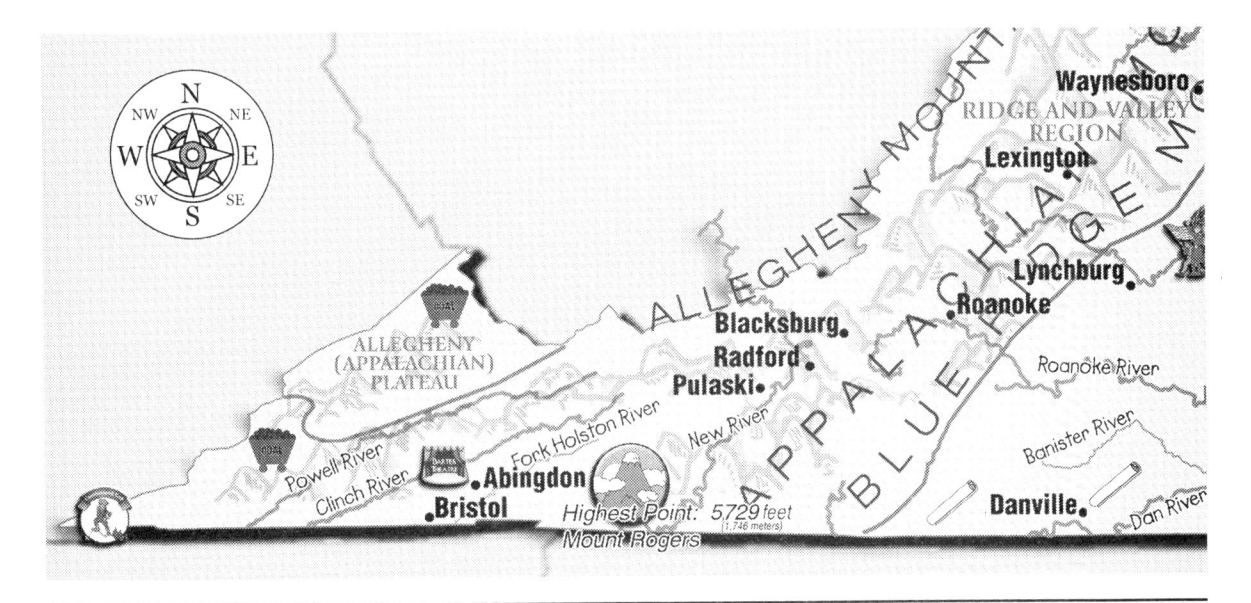

MAP KEY

Coal

Circle the symbols for coal on the map.

2. The area of Virginia known for coal mining is:
    A. Eastern Virginia
    B. Northern Virginia
    C. Southwest Virginia

Hampton Roads

The area of Virginia known as Hampton Roads sounds like it might be a place of many highways. However, it is most known for:

- its deep harbor which can hold large ships
- its excellent location on the James River
- its shipbuilding industry

Look at the map below to answer the questions.

1. Into what large body of water does the James River flow?.

   A. Potomac River
   B. Great Dismal Swamp
   C. Chesapeake Bay

2. Shipbuilding is done:

   A. In inland communities
   B. In waterside communities
   C. In mountain communities

3. A large ship can dock and load or unload goods best in a:

   A. poultry plant
   B. apple orchard
   C. deep harbor

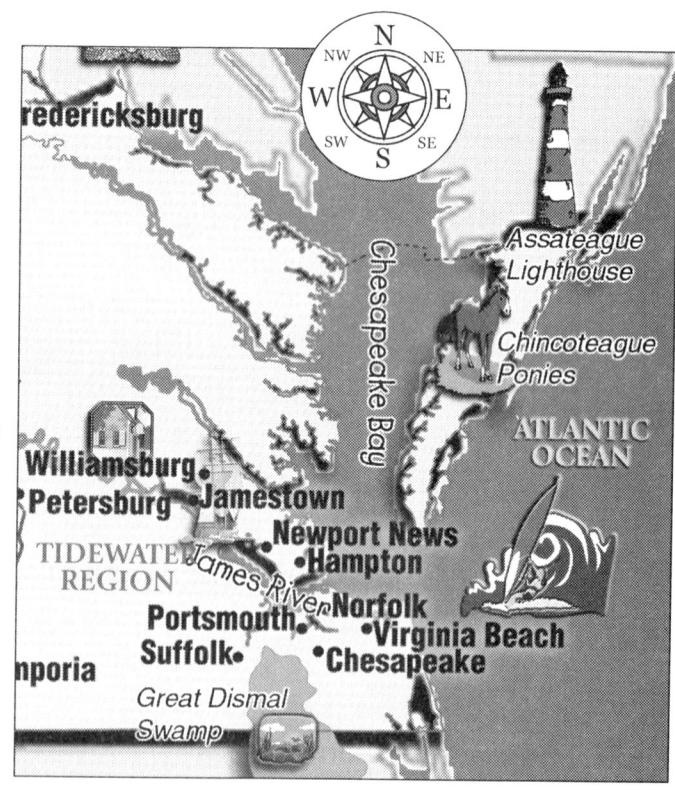

Identifying Virginia Communities!

Use the map below to answer the questions. Circle the correct letter or letters that correspond to the letters on the map.

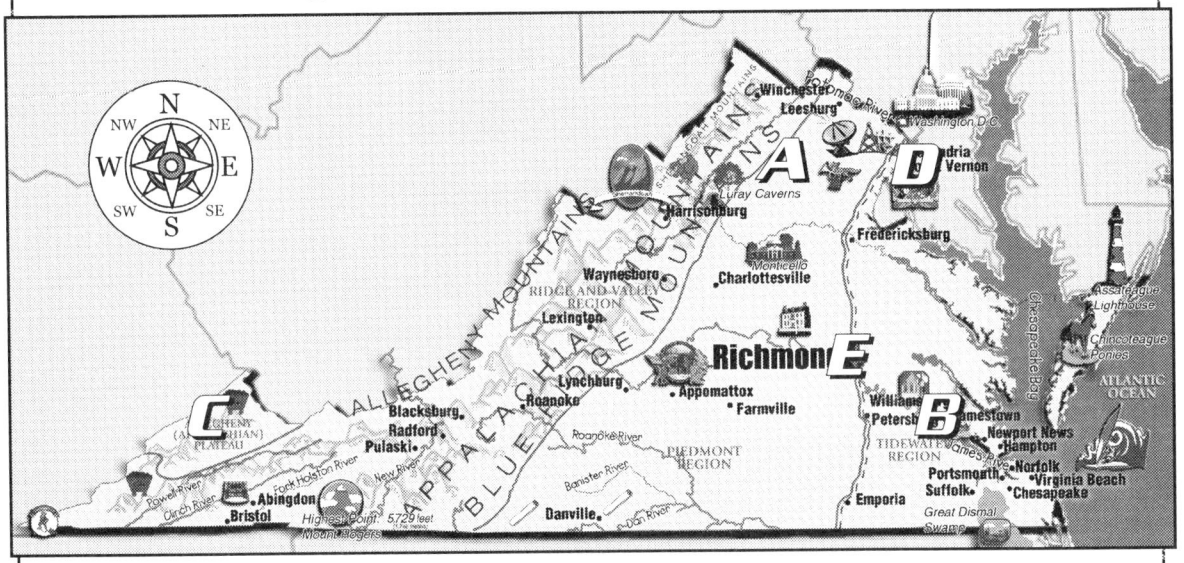

1. Richmond and Hampton Roads are both located on this body of water.   A   B   C   D   E

2. Caverns and orchards are most often found in this area.   A   B   C   D   E

3. The fall line runs through this city.   A   B   C   D   E

4. Coal mining is done in the mountains of this area of Virginia   A   B   C   D   E

5. Many U.S. government office are located in this part of Virginia.   A   B   C   D   E

A Quick Review for YOU!

A. Circle the type of architecture you can find in the city of Richmond and in the office areas of Northern Virginia.

B. Circle the area where you are most likely to find caverns.

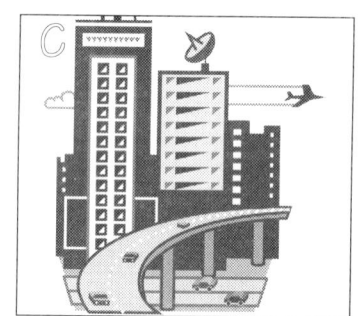

C. Circle the place most likely to have a low population density.

And One More for Fun!

Match the things on the left looking for a home on the right!

1. Runaway chicken   A. Hampton Roads harbor

2. Floundering fish   B. Shenandoah Valley coop

3. Ship at sea   C. The Metro

4. Lost commuter   D. Eastern Shore net

5. Sidetracked coal car   E. Southwest mountain railroad

4.2d Virginia and the United States are divided into regions.

Virginia's Four Regions!

Virginia is divided into four geographic regions. These are:

Tidewater
Piedmont
Ridge and Valley
Allegheny (Appalachian) Plateau

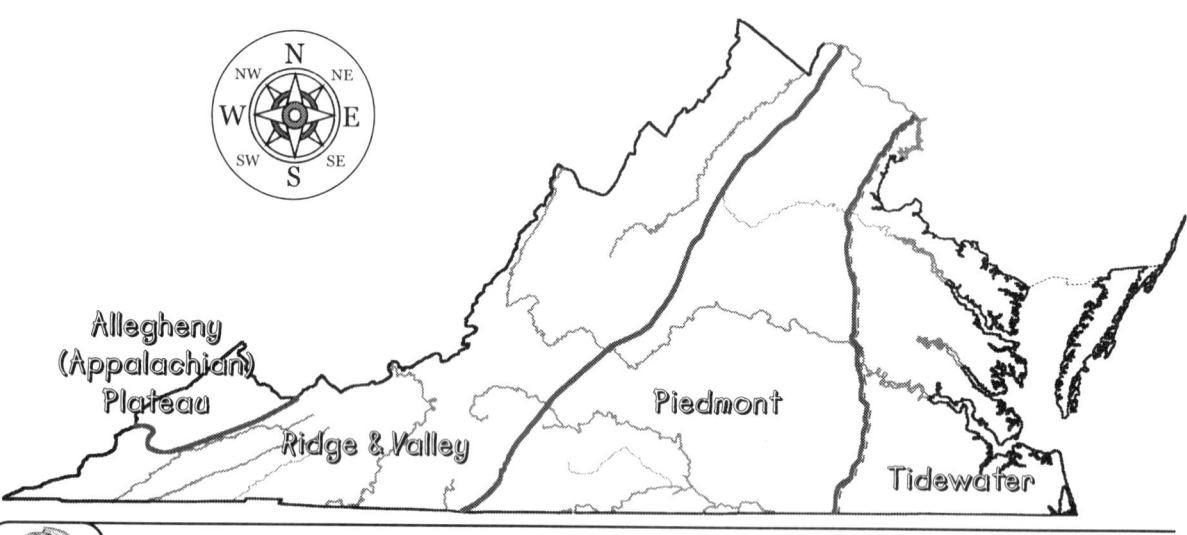

Region	Type of Land	Land Use
Tidewater	Flat land, coastal plain	Vegetable & tobacco farming, fishing, shipbuilding
Piedmont	Rolling hills, plateau	Lumbering and farming
Ridge & Valley	Mountains and valleys	Livestock, fruit, and poultry farming
Allegheny (Appalachian) Plateau	High plateau	Coal mining

Have You Had Your Physical?

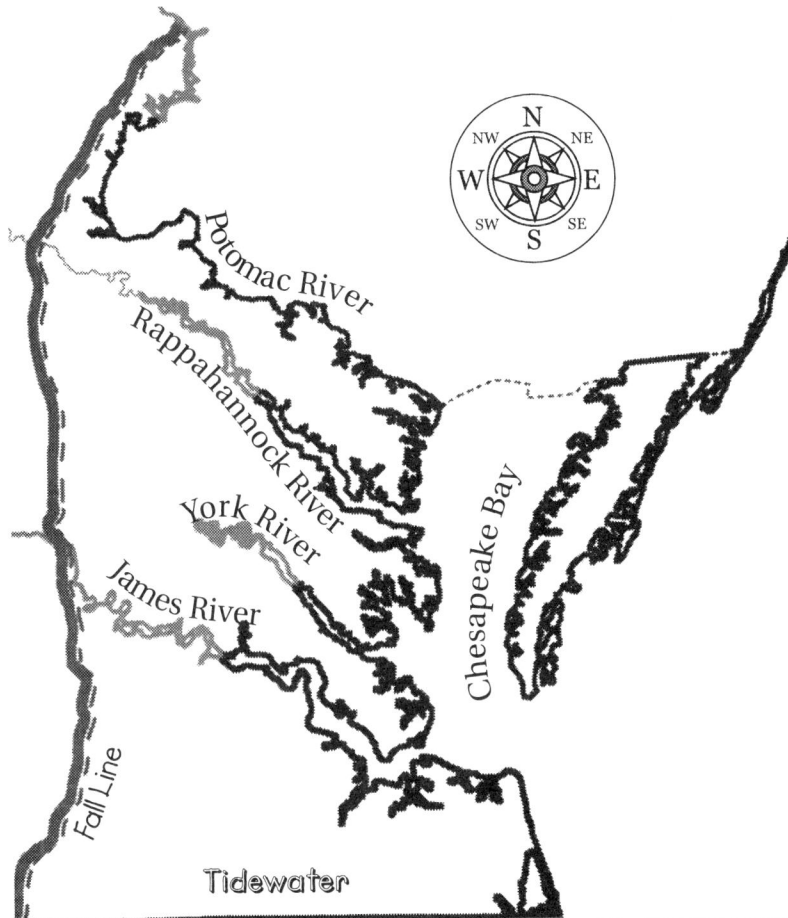

Each of Virginia's four regions has its own physical characteristics. Let's take a look!

The **Tidewater** region's most prominent physical features are:
- It is a coastal plain, or flat land, beside coastal waters
- It includes the large body of water called the Chesapeake Bay
- The James, York, Rappahannock, and Potomac Rivers are located here

Use the map above to answer these questions:

1. The Tidewater's most prominent physical features are:

   A. flat land and water   B. mountains and lakes   C. caverns and orchards

2. The Tidewater is ___ East or ___ West of the fall line.

3. The Chesapeake is a: ___ river or ___ bay.

4. The Tidewater is flat land called a _____ ___ _____.

5. The Rappahannock is a: ___ river or ___ bay.

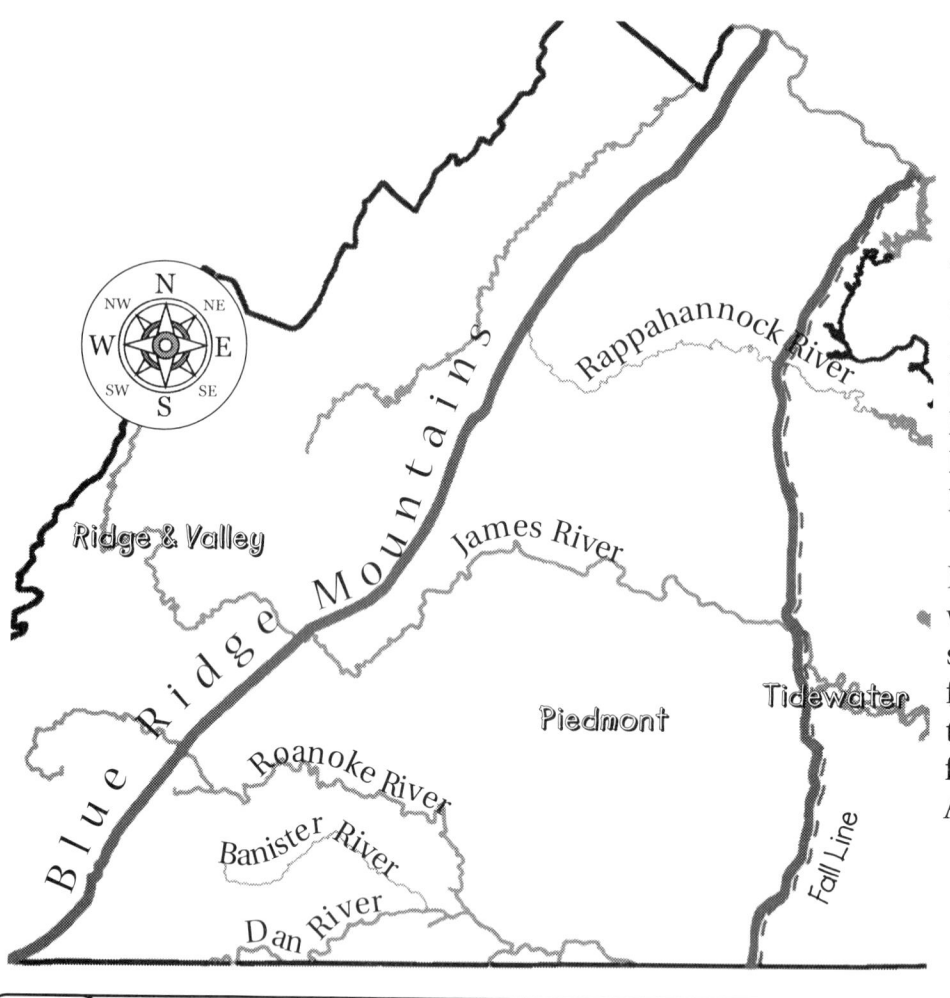

The *Piedmont* is the area of rolling hills between the fall line and the Blue Ridge Mountains.

Rapids occur where the rivers spill over rocky falls and onto the plain to flow toward the Atlantic Ocean.

Use the map above to answer the questions below.

1. The Piedmont is __East or __West of the Tidewater.

2. A plateau is __higher or __lower than a coastal plain.

3. Rapids in the Piedmont flow __east or __west over the fall line.

4. The Ridge & Valley region is __ east or __ west of the Piedmont region.

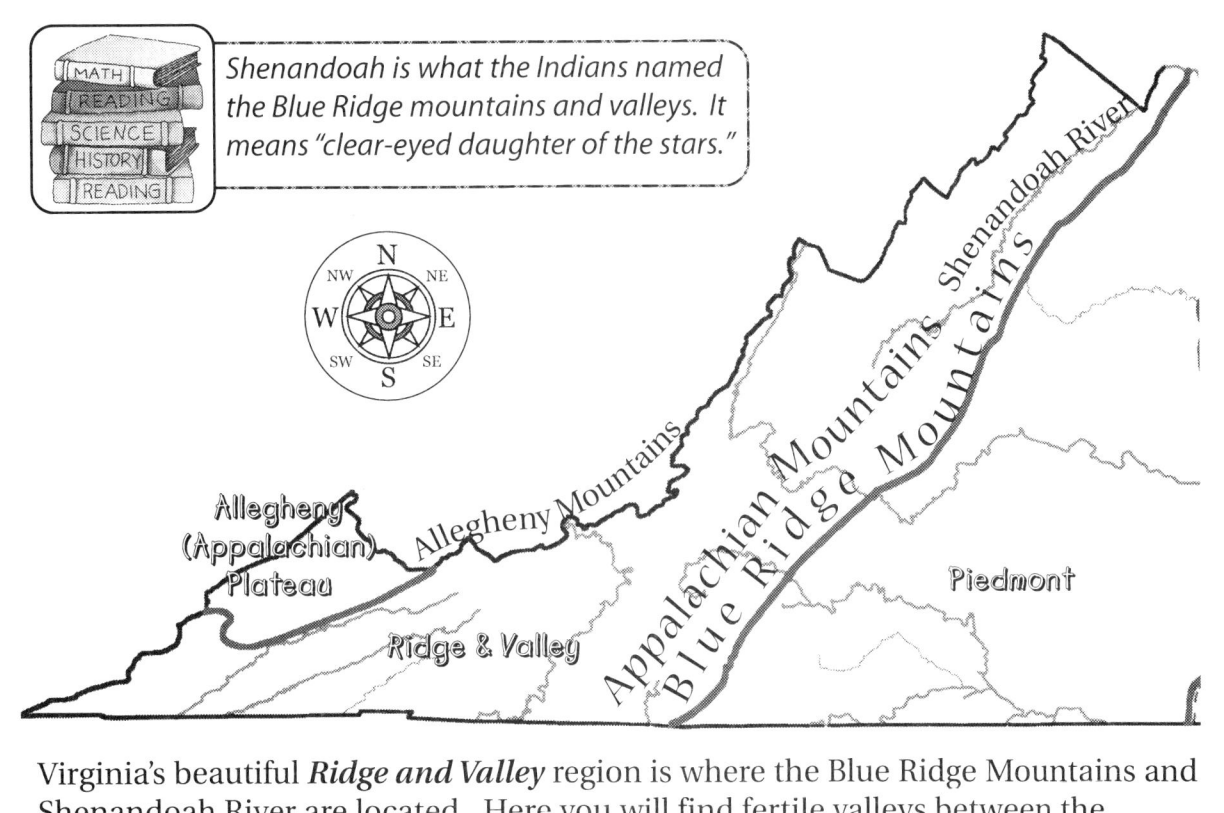

Shenandoah is what the Indians named the Blue Ridge mountains and valleys. It means "clear-eyed daughter of the stars."

Virginia's beautiful **Ridge and Valley** region is where the Blue Ridge Mountains and Shenandoah River are located. Here you will find fertile valleys between the mountain ranges and caverns beneath the earth.

The Blue Ridge Mountains run from Georgia, through our neighboring state of North Carolina, up into the southwestern corner of Virginia and keep going until they reach the northern tip of the state, just a few miles west of Washington, D.C. The Blue Ridge gets its name from the bluish appearance of the trees from a distance.

1. The Blue Ridge Mountains run:
　　__ northeast and southwest　or　__ east and west

2. The Piedmont region is __ west or __ east of the Blue Ridge Mountains.

3. The _____ River is located in the Ridge & Valley region.

4. In the Ridge & Valley region, you find _____ valleys and _____ beneath the earth.

The *Allegheny (Appalachian) Plateau* region is an area noted for its coal deposits.

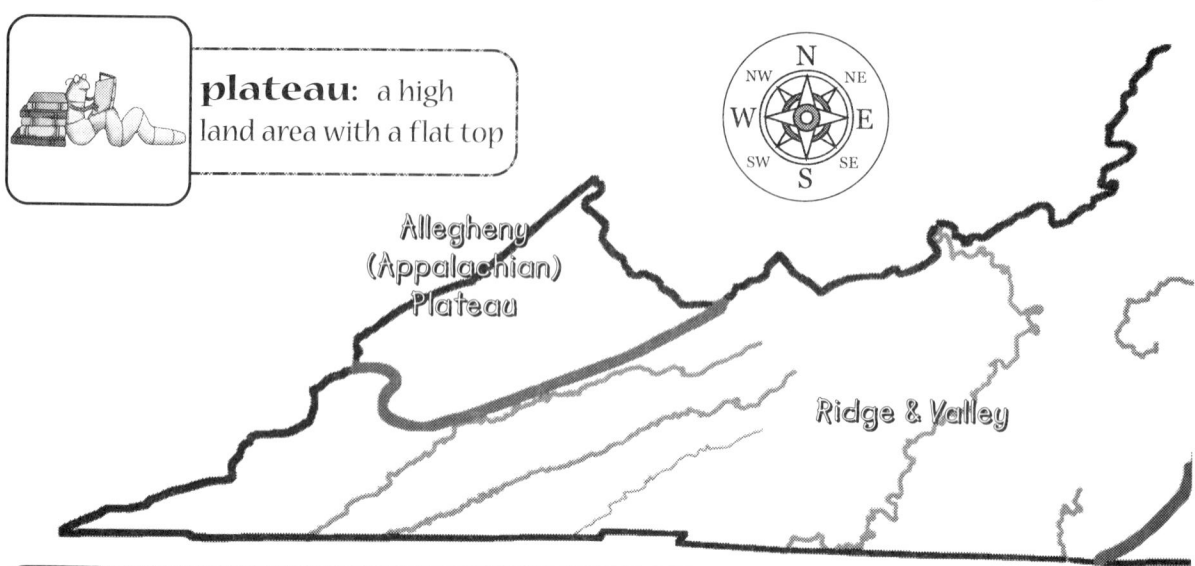

plateau: a high land area with a flat top

Use the map to answer the following questions:

1. The Allegheny (Appalachian) Plateau region is located in this part of Virginia:

   A. Northeast   B. Southwest   C. Southeast   D. Northwest

2. The Allegheny (Appalachian) Plateau region is noted for its _____ _____.

3. The Allegheny (Appalachian) Plateau region is __ east or __ west of the Ridge & Valley, Piedmont, and Tidewater regions.

Black Gold
Rich deposits of coal were discovered in southwestern Virginia in the 1880s. The coalfields of southwestern Virginia are still important to the state's economy. At least 14 million tons of coal were once mined by around 4,500 miners in 300 different mines in Lee, Scott, and Wise counties. Coal is still an important Virginia natural resource.

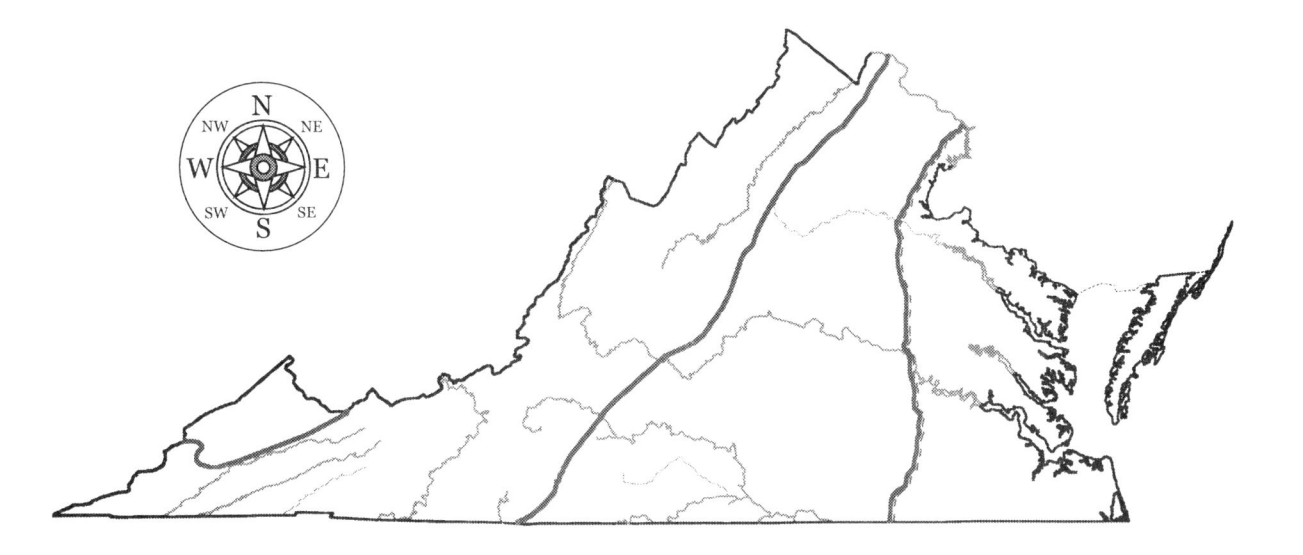

1. What is the name of the region in Virginia's southwest corner?:
    A. Ridge and Valley
    B. Allegheny (Appalachian) Plateau

2. Label the Tidewater region on the map.

3. What is the name of the region just west of the Tidewater?:

    _____

4. What is the name of the peninsula just off Virginia's shore?
    A. Atlantic Ocean
    B. Maryland
    C. Eastern Shore
    D. Chesapeake Bay

Regions of the United States

The United States can be divided into seven regions. These are:

Coastal Plain
Appalachian Mountains
Interior Lowlands
Great Plains
Rocky Mountains
Basin and Ridge
Coastal Range

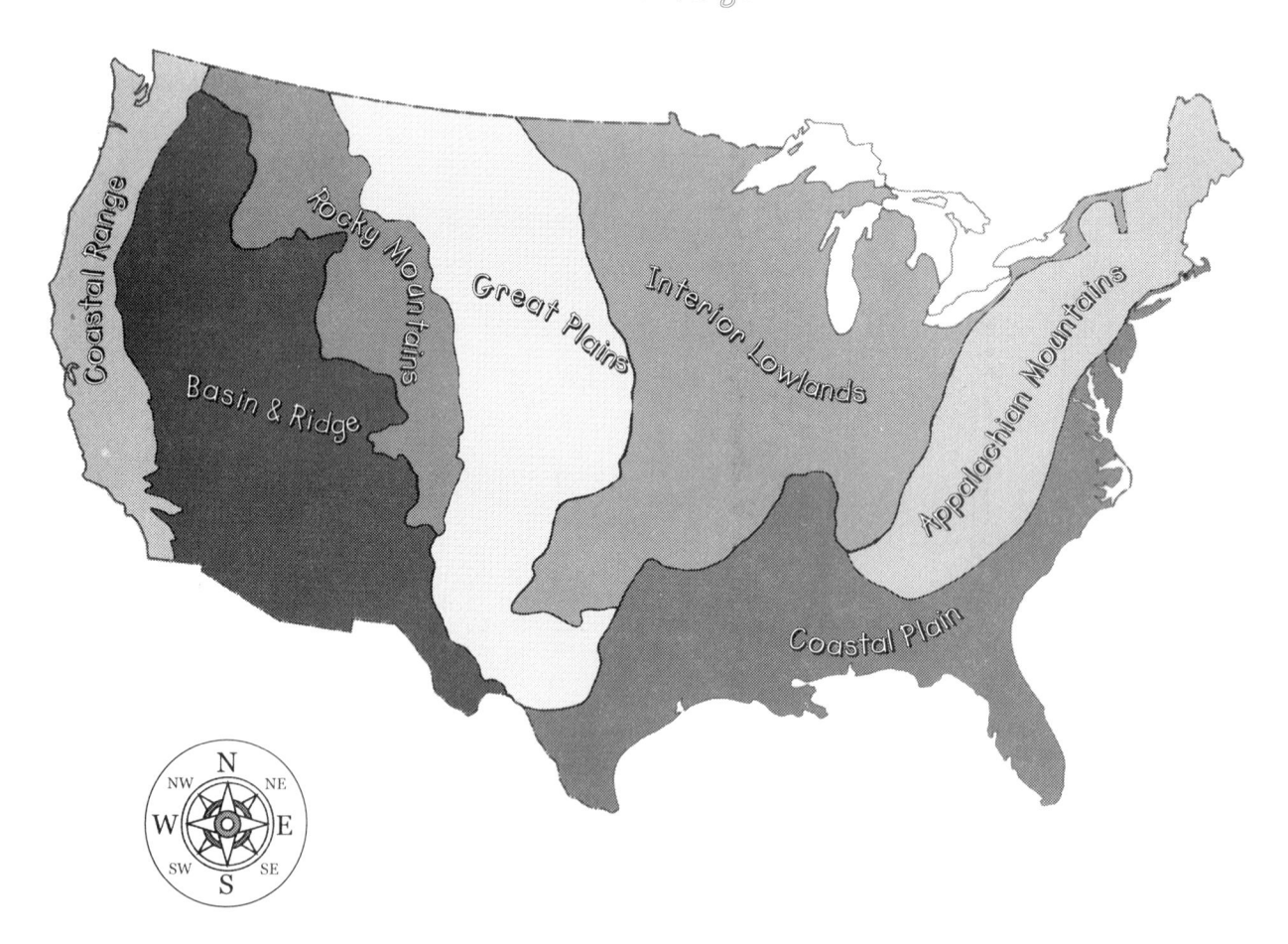

Let's look at the physical characteristics of the seven regions of the United States.

1 Coastal Plain: This flatland is located along the Atlantic Ocean.

2 Appalachian Mountains: This is an area of low, rounded mountains, rivers, and forests.

3 Interior Lowlands: This region has low, flat plains. It is located west of the Appalachian Mountains and east of the Great Plains. It has fertile soil.

4 Great Plains: This flatland has an elevation higher than the Interior Lowlands. It also is known for its fertile soil.

5 Rocky Mountains: These rugged mountains are where the Continental Divide is located. It is a region with a high elevation.

6 Basin and Ridge: This region with a high elevation is on a plateau.

7 Coastal Range: This region has rugged mountains and forests.

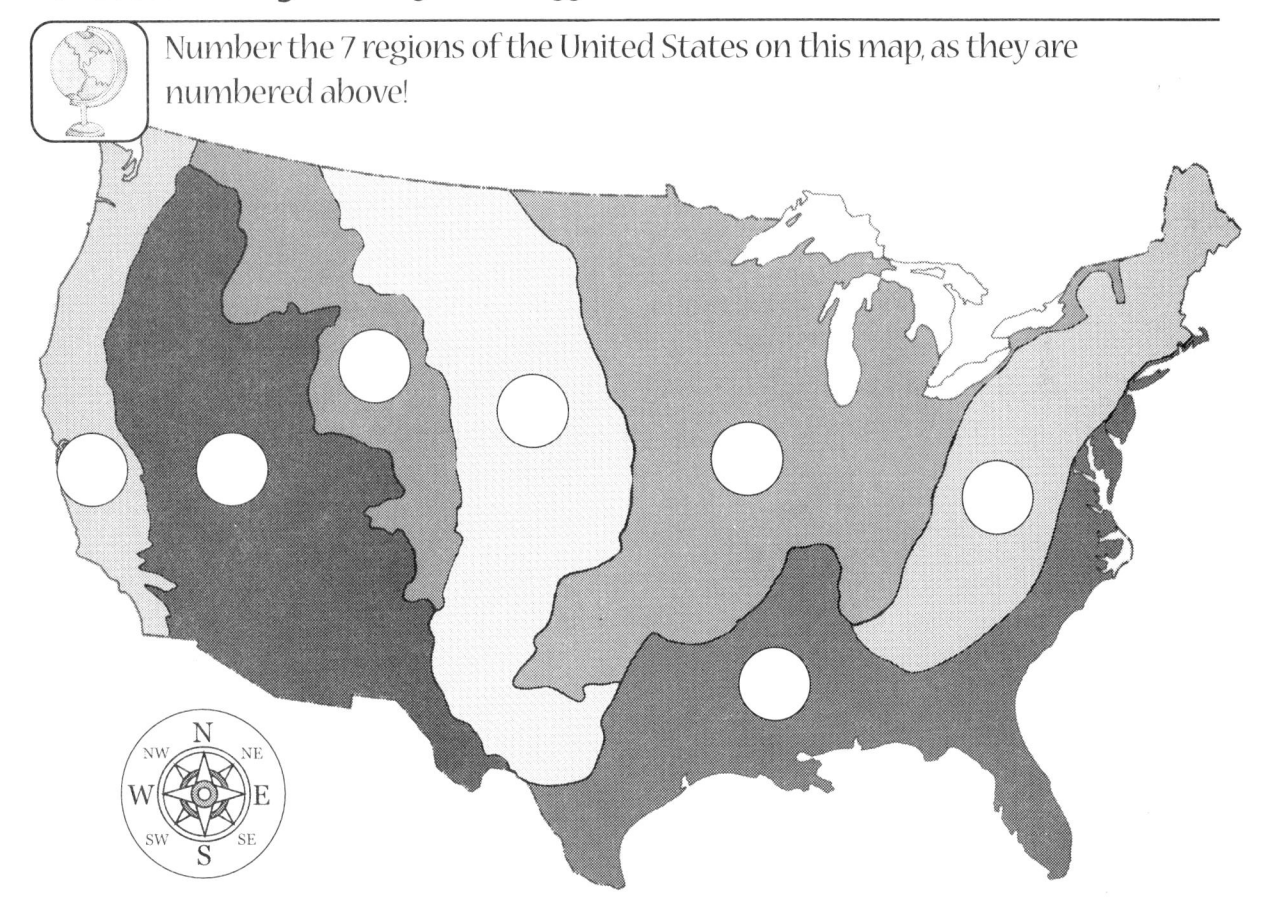

Number the 7 regions of the United States on this map, as they are numbered above!

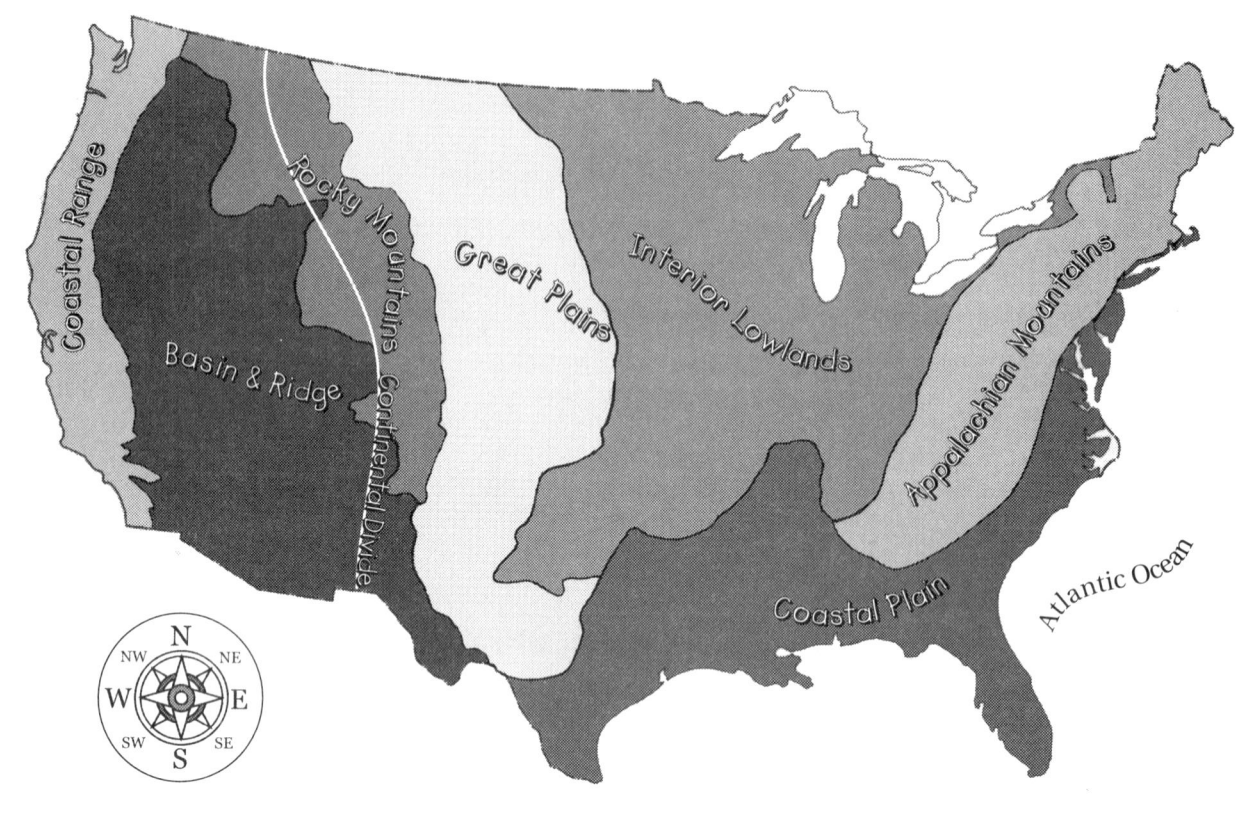

Answer these questions, using the map above:

1. Which region extends the furthest east?

    A. Interior Lowlands   B. Coastal Plain   C. Appalachian Mountains

2. This region is the westernmost region in the U.S.: _____ _____

3. Which region is mountainous?:

    A. Coastal Plain   B. Great Plains   C. Coastal Range

4. The Atlantic Ocean runs beside this region: _____ _____

5. The Continental Divide runs through these regions:

    _____ _____

    _____ _____

Map Key: Forests | Fertile Soil

Use the map and map key to answer these questions:

1. Which two regions are known for fertile soil?:

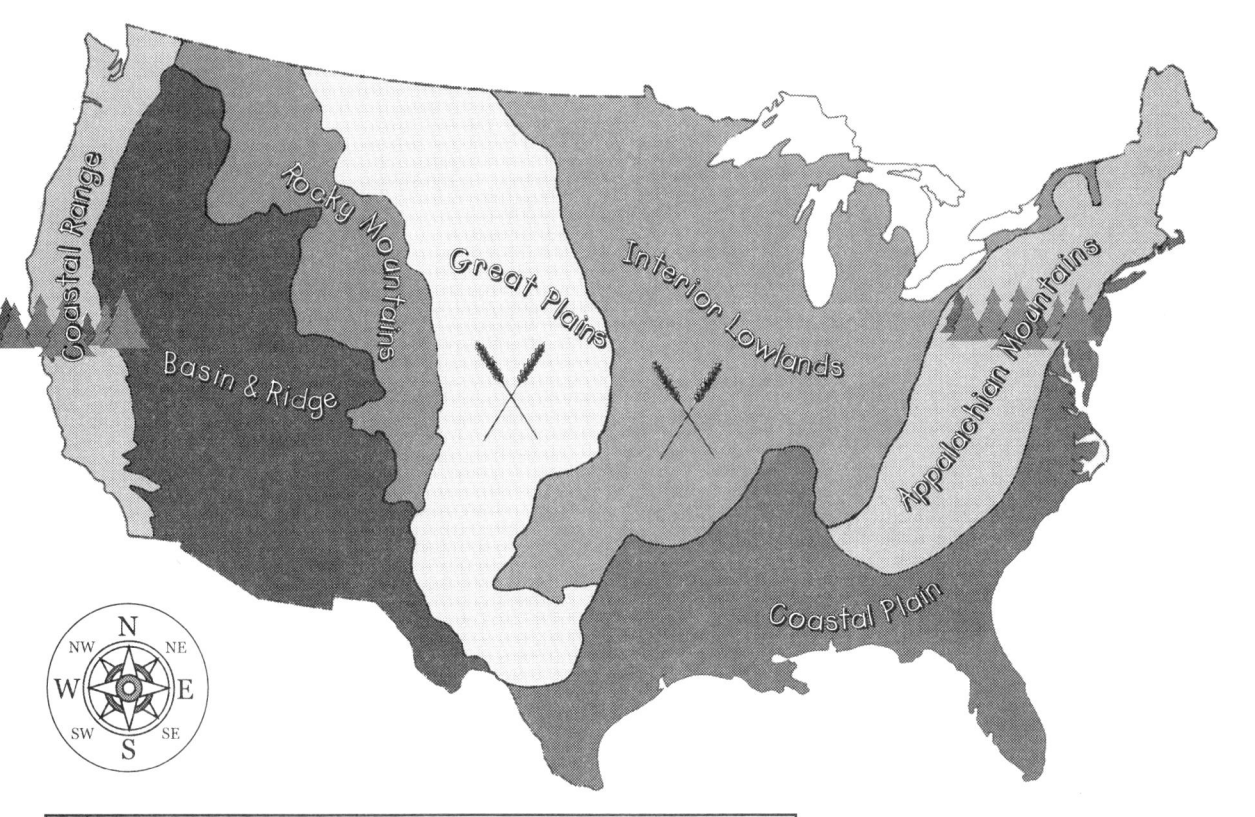

   A. Coastal Plain B. Interior Lowlands
   C. Great Plains   D. Basin and Ridge

2. Which two regions have large amounts of forests?:

   A. Appalachian Mountains B. Great Plains
   C. Rocky Mountains   D. Coastal Range

A Quick Review for YOU!

Match the Virginia region on the left with its description on the right.

1. Allegheny (Appalachian) Plateau
2. Ridge and Valley
3. Piedmont
4. Tidewater

A. Coal deposits
B. Fall line
C. Coastal plain
D. Mountains, valleys, and caverns

Match the U.S. region on the left with its description on the right.

1. Coastal Plain
2. Appalachian Mountains
3. Interior Lowlands
4. Great Plains
5. Rocky Mountains
6. Basin and Ridge
7. Coastal Range

A. Rugged mountains and forests
B. Flatland, fertile soil
C. Continental Divide located here
D. Low flat plains and fertile soil
E. Plateau with high elevation
F. Flatland on the Atlantic Ocean
G. Low mountains, rivers, and forests

One More - Just for Fun!

This Way? Or That Way? *Pretend you are standing smack in the middle of the Mississippi River (on the X on the map below).*

Circle the correct arrow to show which direction you should head to do the following:

                                                    Go West!   Go East!

1. To go swim in the Atlantic Ocean   ⇐   ⇒

2. To return to the state of Virginia   ⇐   ⇒

3. To see how the corn's growing in the Great Plains   ⇐   ⇒

4. To stand on the Continental Divide   ⇐   ⇒

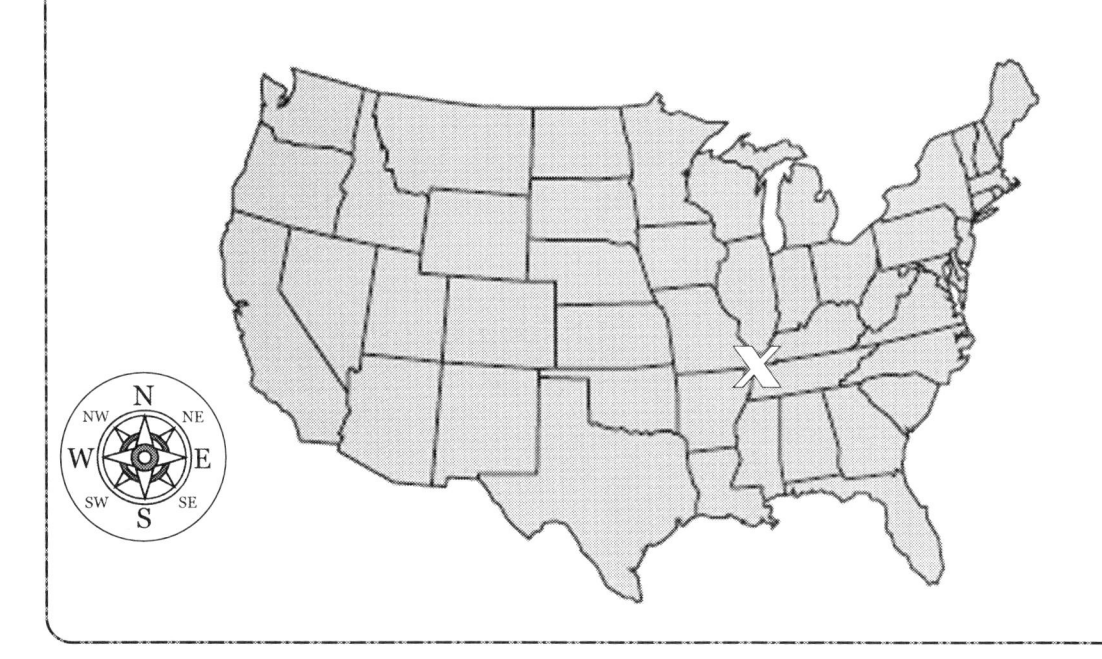

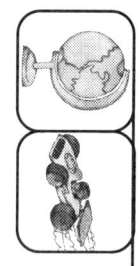

This one's ALL for fun! See if you can find the Virginia cities and landmarks in the Word Search! (Hints: the first or last letter of the city name rests NEAR the actual spot where you would find the city on a real map; other names are hidden both on and off the map. So, if you know your geography, this will take no time at all!)

Allegheny Appalachian
Plateau
Alexandria
Appomattox
Blue Ridge Mountains
Bristol
Charlottesville
Chesapeake Bay
Danville
Emporia
Fall Line
Fredericksburg
Harrisonburg
James River
Jamestown
Leesburg
Lexington
Lynchburg
Richmond
Monticello
Mount Rogers
Mount Vernon
Norfolk
Piedmont
Potomac
Ridge and Valley
Roanoke
Shenandoah
Tidewater
Waynesboro
Williamsburg
Winchester

```
R V P I E D M O N T D J S V S M C J S D Y S K F K B M X M S G P W R I G V N
I S A B S G M R U J F J D D S W I N C H E S T E R E O F J F O I L J V H C
D H S F H E O A N D A H E J H W O L E E S B U R G E S T L R A K X H
G N D A G H U S H E N A N D O A H F T R H A L E X A N D R I A O L I M G T E
E D D L S A N A L W J V L A S D G V B M O U N T V E R N O N M I K E O H S
A K S L E K T K N A S H A R R I S O N B U R G W J V K S D F G A A G S S J A
N I A L V B R S H T J B M F J S F R E D E R I C K S B U R G C M V R R K P
D S K I B L O D K E G W A Y N E S B O R O C C H A R L O T T E S V I L L E
V D J N Y S G E U R J L E X I N G T O N G I M O N T I C E L L O B D V G H A
A L L E G H E N Y A P P A L A C H I A N P L A T E A U I D T V U D E D K
L Q Q W J B R H X F D M N H J F Y T B H R I C H M O N D F G A R S R K K E
L H F G Y T S J H O P L Y N C H B U R G Y A P P O M A T T O X F G V B C F B
E O O H P R I U D R O A N O K E F O F A S D E J A M E S T O W N E G M M A
Y D F Y K H G J B L U E R I D G E M O U N T A I N S G T N O R F O L K G U Y
J B R I S T O L B K V L D A N V I L L E S J E M P O R I A U R E P O I L F H
```

Section 2

History, Economics, and Civics

Virginia had the first representative assembly in the New World. Virginia was the first American colony to declare itself independent from the British king. Virginia is one of only four states that calls itself a "commonwealth," which means "united for the common good."

Chapter 1

Many of Virginia's first leaders were reluctant heroes. George Mason would have preferred staying home to his life in politics. He and Patrick Henry opposed the Constitution because they said it did not give enough power to the people. George Washington refused pay for serving as Commander-in-Chief of the Continental Army during the Revolutionary War. He had to be convinced to serve as the chairman of the Constitutional Convention of 1787.

4.3a - Virginia was a new colony. It established an economic, social, and political life. However, it continued to have a strong relationship to its parent country of England. Like a child trying to grow up and live on its own, this was bound to cause conflict!

The Virginia Company of London and the Virginia Colony

The Virginia colony was established by the Virginia Company of London, England. The Virginia Company began the Virginia colony as an economic venture.

colony: a group of people who settle in a distant territory but remain subject to (ruled by) their parent country

Check which came first:

___The Virginia Colony   ___The Virginia Company of London

If you participate in an economic venture, you hope to:

___A. make money
___B. lose money

Economic Interdependence

The Virginia colony and England were economically interdependent. England depended on raw materials exported from the Virginia colony. The Virginia colony depended on imported manufactured goods from England.

economics: the science that deals with the production, distribution, and consumption of goods and services

1. An example of economic interdependence is:

___A. You are independently wealthy.
___B. You trade vegetables that you have grown in your garden for some homemade bread from a neighbor.

Raw materials exported from the Virginia colony to England included wood used for shipbuilding. Manufactured goods imported from England to the Virginia colony included clothing, iron pots, and tools.

2. Raw materials are:

___A. uncooked
___B. clothing
___C. things used to make a final product

3. Manufactured goods are:

___A. made from raw materials
___B. found in the earth

If you *import* something, it comes to you from somewhere else.
If you *export* something, you send it to another place.

4. What was the economic relationship between the Virginia colony and England?

A. England depended on _____ _____ exported from the Virginia colony.

B. The Virginia colony depended on _____ _____ imported from England.

English Law Rules!

England and the Virginia colony not only had an economic relationship, but a political relationship as well. The Virginia colony, though far away from its parent country, was subject to (had to obey) English law.

politics: the activities related to a government

Pretend that you have left your country and moved across a large body of water to a new place. The leaders in your country want to continue to tell you what to do, even though they are not there to see what your life is like. How do you feel about this?

_____
_____
_____
_____
_____
_____
_____
_____
_____
_____

Fill in the blanks.

1. The Virginia colony was subject to _____ law.

2. England and the Virginia colony had an economic relationship and a _____ relationship.

Virginia Establishes Its Own Government

Although people in the Virginia colony did not always like being subject to the laws of a faraway country, they respected the system of government that they had always known. So, perhaps it is not surprising that when the Virginia colony established its own government, it was modeled after the representative government they had known in England.

A *representative government* is one in which a few people represent or carry out the wishes of all the people.

1. How did early Virginians show respect for the English form of government?

___A. They ignored it.
___B. They copied certain ideas and systems in their new government.

Write E if the phrase describes England.
Write A if the phrase describes America.
Write B if the phrase describes both England and America.

_____ 2. They were economically interdependent
_____ 3. Voters elect representatives
_____ 4. Imported manufactured goods
_____ 5. Founded colonies across the ocean
_____ 6. Was subject to laws from its parent country

The House of Burgesses

The House of Burgesses was the first representative government in the Virginia colony. It was also the first representative government in North and South America. Today, it is called the General Assembly. It is the oldest legislative body in the western hemisphere.

1. Virginia is part of the United States. The United States is part of:

__North America __South America

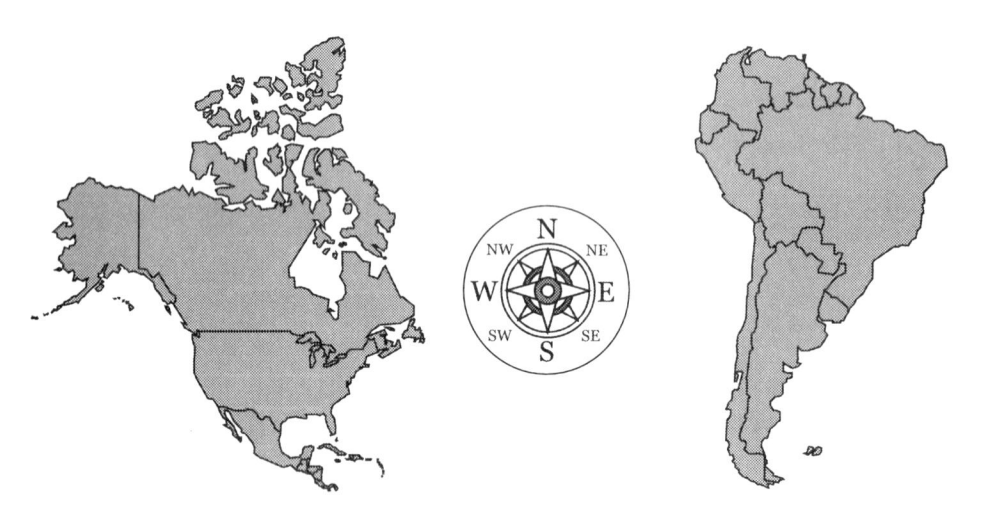

2. Virginia is located in the:

__eastern hemisphere __western hemisphere

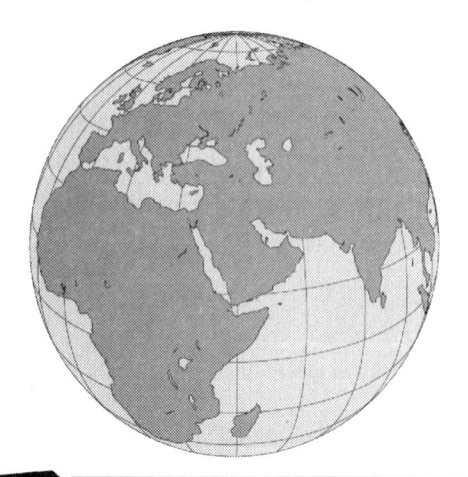

Conflict!

Conflict developed between England and the Virginia colony over several things. One of these was *taxation*. Another was the *lack of representation* in the English government.

The Virginia colonists did not think that it was fair that they had to pay taxes to their mother country but were not represented in England's government.

More conflict developed between England and the Virginia colony over who would pay for the French and Indian War.

As you might imagine, these conflicts led to disagreements and the desire of the Virginia colonists to be independent from England, govern themselves, and live their lives as they wanted in the New World.

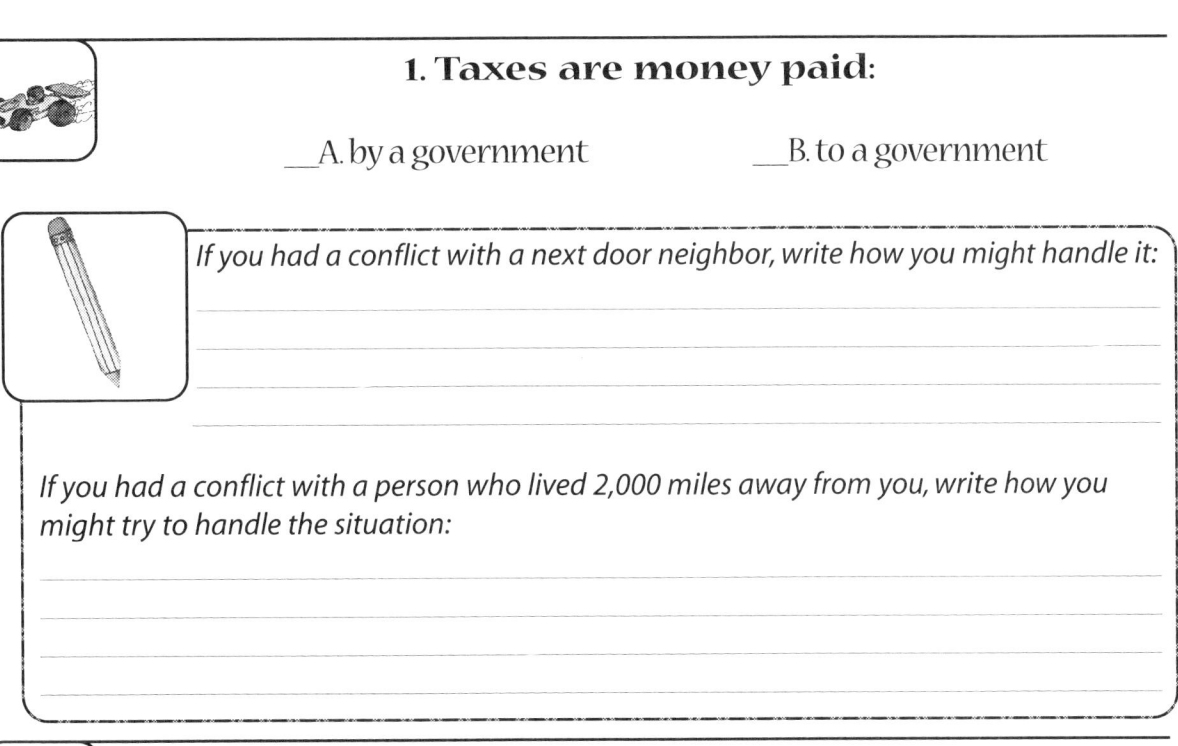

---

1. Taxes are money paid:

___A. by a government   ___B. to a government

If you had a conflict with a next door neighbor, write how you might handle it:

_____
_____
_____

If you had a conflict with a person who lived 2,000 miles away from you, write how you might try to handle the situation:

_____
_____
_____
_____

Because colonists and the English could not agree:

A. The colonists went home to England.
B. The colonists wanted to make their own laws.

The French and Indian War

The countries of England and France were in a race to control the Ohio Valley. The French had begun to build a chain of forts between Lake Erie and the Ohio River. A twenty-one-year-old Virginian knew this territory well because he had surveyed land in the region. His name was George Washington. He was sent to persuade the French to stop building the forts. When they refused, he led a troop of 150 men in an attack on one of the forts. This began the French and Indian War of 1754-1763. George Washington won this first battle, but was later defeated in another skirmish. However, with the help of the colonists, England won this war.

I Remember England!

The Virginia colonists brought very little with them to the New World. This is one reason that they had such a difficult time getting settled in Jamestown. However, they were influenced by their former lives in England as they began to establish their own culture and society in this new, raw land.

Cultural and social influences from England included: religion, language, architecture, fashion, and family structure.

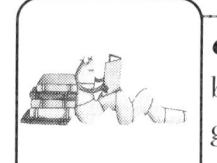

culture: the general behavior and lifestyle of a group of people

society: a group of people with a common culture or way of life

Imagine that you have moved halfway around the world to a place new to you. Make a list of the things that you would miss from your former life:

_____   _____

_____   _____

_____   _____

Religion: Some colonists came to the New World in search of religious freedom. Religion was important in daily life. Houses of worship played an important role in the community. Religious leaders conducted baptisms, weddings, and funerals. Since there was little leisure time for hard-working colonists, Sunday was the one day that they could look forward to rest and worship.

Religious life in the Virginia colony was influenced by England. The first English settlers designated the Church of England as their established church. Dissenters included the Puritans and Quakers, two small groups who did not accept the established church.

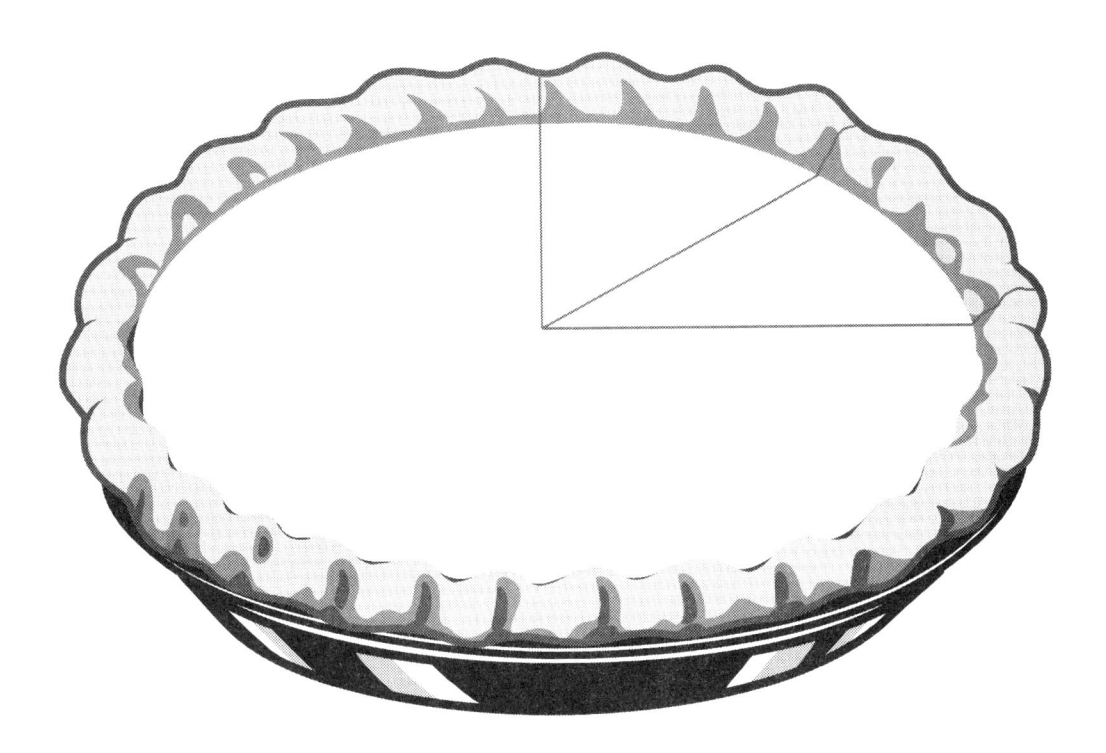

On the "pie" chart above, label each wedge with the name of the church or religious groups that came from England to the Virginia colony.

Language: While the Virginia colonists certainly spoke the English language, it sounded quite different than the English we hear spoken today. Even today you can still hear a little of the unique Elizabethan accent spoken by some older people, especially in the Tidewater region and on the Eastern Shore. Some old English words include: arn (iron), cider (fruit juice), and salat (salad).

Do You Speak the Language?

Using the word bank below, see if you can translate the paragraph from "Old English" to today's English!

balloo - a game of ball
costardmonger - apple seller
mammothrept - spoiled child
strummel patched - long, loose, tangled hair

Old English

After the children finished their lessons and chores, they would go outside to play balloo. They played balloo in the street, and often knocked down the costardmonger. Whenever Sam lost the game, he would act like a mammothrept. And Molly would be scolded by her mother for coming home with strummel patched.

Today's English

Architecture: The houses the early Virginia colonists built were simple structures for protection against the weather and Indian attacks. They were made of materials at hand, such as mud and rough wood. Later, as bigger and fancier buildings were constructed in Williamsburg, the colonists copied ideas from the homes back in England. Some of these buildings were made of brick and wood by talented masons and carpenters. We still see examples of English architecture in America today.

Using the diagrams below, answer the following questions:

1. Early colonists' houses were for protection against _____ and _____ _____.

2. Houses built later were copied from homes back in _____.

3. Buildings in Williamsburg were made of _____ and _____.

Early Colonists' Houses
- Simple structures
- Made of mud and rough wood
- Protection from weather and Indian attacks

Colonists' Houses Built Later
- Bigger and fancier
- Made of brick and wood
- Copied from homes in England

Fashion: Colonists dressed much as they had back in England. Working men wore knee-length breeches with long stockings, shirts, and vests. Women wore skirts, called petticoats, and blouses. They tied a pouch on a string around their waist over their apron to serve as a "pocket." Women generally wore mob caps of white cloth, often beneath a straw hat. Women wore hats indoors and out. In Williamsburg, you might have seen men in wigs wearing three-cornered cocked (tricorn) hats. These were often decorated with ostrich plumes or pheasant feathers and colorful ribbon rosettes called cockades. Children dressed much like adults! I'll bet they would have liked tee shirts!

Draw a line from each word to its correct place on the characters.

petticoat

tricorn hat

mob cap

blouse

stockings

apron

wig

breeches

Family Structure: For most colonists, life centered around the family. A colonial child was likely to share his or her home not only with parents, sisters, and brothers, but possibly also with a grandparent, unmarried aunt or uncle, an orphan cousin, and perhaps even a brother's or sister's wife or husband and their children! These large families were an economic necessity. Many hands could help with the many chores. Everyone contributed to make the family self-sufficient.

1. Being self-sufficient means:
A. Dependent on others
B. Able to take care of oneself

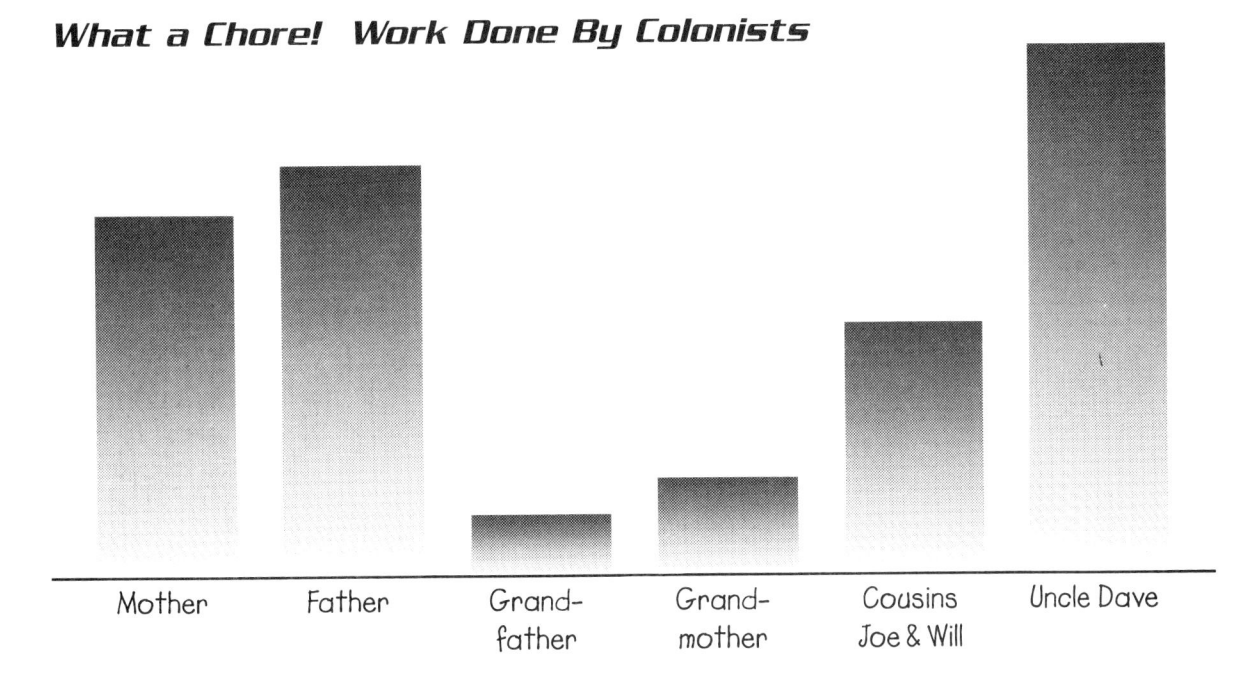

What a Chore! Work Done By Colonists

Mother | Father | Grand-father | Grand-mother | Cousins Joe & Will | Uncle Dave

Using the information provided on the graph, answer the following questions:

2. Which colonist did the most chores?: _____
3. Which colonist did the least chores?: _____
4. Which two colonists worked as a team to get their chores done?
_____ and _____

Many families today are ____ larger or ____ smaller than colonial families.

How many people are in your family? _____

How many other students in your class have the same number of people in their families? _____

Look at the three items below. Circle which you think would have the most value to you as a colonist. Write one sentence saying why this is so.

Tobacco

Food

Shoes

_____
_____
_____
_____

A Quick Review for YOU!

1. Virginia began as an _____ colony.
2. The Virginia colony and England were economically inter-_____.
3. The Virginia colony's government was based on the English model of a _____ government.
4. The House of _____ was the first representative government in America.

One More - Just for Fun!

You are a young Virginia colonist. It has been a busy Monday. There was corn to be harvested, you had to help with the baby, and chop wood for the fire. Write your daily diary entry here:

_____
_____
_____
_____
_____
_____
_____
_____
_____

4.3b - Many types of people contributed to the economic, social, and political life of the Virginia colony.

Everyone Contributes!

Many different groups of people made important contributions to the development of the Virginia colony.

The different groups of people who contributed to the success of the Virginia colony included the American Indians, the English, the Germans, Scotch-Irish, and the African slaves.

contribute: to help, to take part in, to do your share

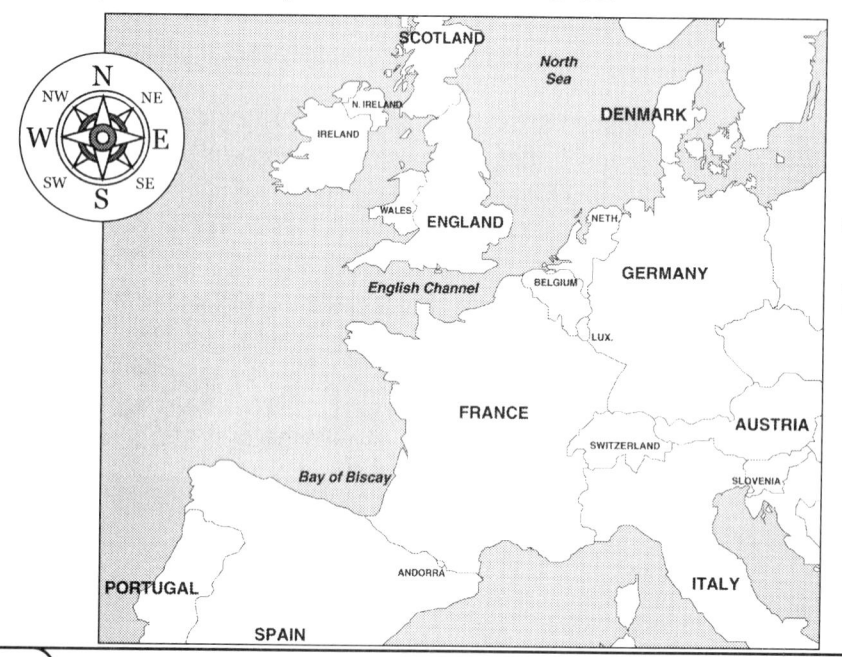

Where did people in colonial Virginia come from? The American Indians were already living on the land.

Using the map above, complete this Quick Quiz:

1. Circle the countries that sent settlers to Virginia.

2. Underline the name of the country whose settlers landed in Jamestown first.

3. Find the ocean European settlers had to cross to get to America. Write its name in the correct area.

Making a Contribution!

These groups made important contributions to the Virginia colony:

American Indians

strategy: a plan of action, a way to get things done

• American Indian tribes taught colonists survival strategies.

Because the Indians taught the colonists strategic skills, the colonists were able to survive.

Match the skill taught with the result.

1. How to grow crops 
2. How to store crops through the winter 
3. How to hunt game

A. They had meat to eat.
B. They harvested food to eat. 
C. They did not starve.

English

- Members of the Virginia Company of London financed the establishment of the Virginia colony.

finance: to pay for something

- *Indentured servants* provided an inexpensive source of labor. Indentured servants were people who worked for colonists for a certain period of time to pay off the cost of their passage to the colony.

- Colonial leaders established a representative form of government. This was called the *House of Burgesses*.

---

1. Circle the correct answer:
With the help of indentured servants, plantation owners were able to:

   A. clear more land
   B. grow more crops
   C. make more money
   D. feed more people
   E. A, B, C, and D

2. Circle the correct answer:
In a representative form of government, these people make the rules:

   A. individuals selected by the people to represent them
   B. a king or queen
   C. no one

• Plantation owners cultivated the cash crop of tobacco.

cultivate: to plant, grow, and harvest a crop

Virginia plantation owners sent tobacco back to England. The colonists ate most of the other crops they planted, but tobacco was a ***cash crop***. This meant colonists could exchange tobacco for other goods.

Circle three things that they might have received in return:

• Women established families and educated the children. Families were often very large, with as many as 12-15 or more people living together. Everyone in the family contributed to the daily chores. Children studied reading, writing, and arithmetic.

Circle the type of setting a colonial Virginia child studied in:

Germans/Scotch-Irish

- These settlers farmed the area west of the Blue Ridge Mountains.

Draw a farmhouse on the west side of the Blue Ridge Mountains.

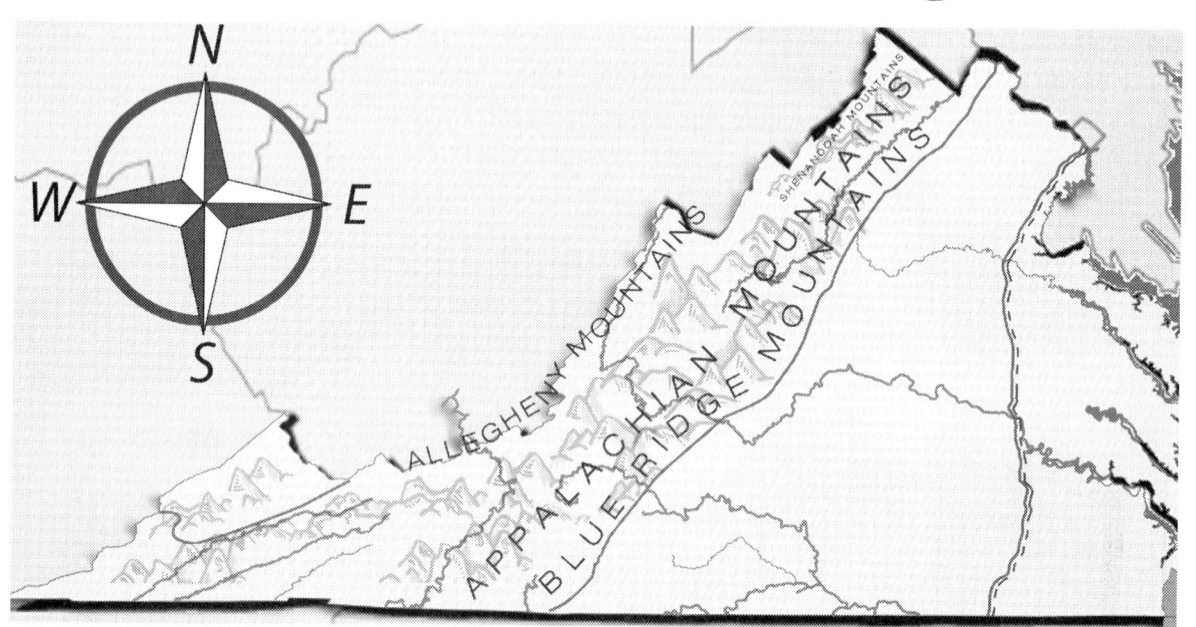

African Slaves

- Slaves provided the main source of labor in cultivating tobacco.

Tobacco in Colonial Virginia

In 1612, Virginia colonist John Rolfe experimented with growing tobacco. Two years later, he learned how to "cure" the green leaves until they were brown. He shipped these dried leaves back to England, where people in fashionable society learned (cough! cough!) to enjoy smoking.

The success of tobacco as a money-making crop was astounding. From four barrels shipped in 1614, the quantity grew to 2,500 pounds (1,125 kilograms), 50,000 pounds (22,500 kilograms), and by 1628, 500,000 pounds (225,000 kilograms)! In addition to making money for the colony, tobacco itself was used as money. In 1619 or 1620, the first English women came to the Jamestown colony as "mail order brides." These brides had a price! A settler had to pay 120 pounds (54 kilograms) of tobacco, the price of a woman's ship passage, to gain the right to say, "I do."

Match the colonial Virginia person below with the letter of the diary entry that they might have made.

1 - slave ___
2 - Virginia Company of London member ___
3 - indentured servant ___
4 - House of Burgesses member ___
5 - plantation owner ___
6 - German/Scotch-Irish farmer ___
7 - mother ___

A - "Another day working to pay off my debt has gone by."

B - "It was a very hot day to pick tobacco!"

C - "The children made good progress in their studies today."

D - "The clouds that came over the Blue Ridge mountains brought rain to our crops today."

E - "I hope there will be enough tobacco for our company to make a profit this year."

F - "No matter how many people I have working on the land, I always seem to need more!"

G - "I think we did a good job representing the people today."

A Quick Review for YOU!

1. The representative form of government was called the _____ of _____.

2. American _____ taught colonists survival strategies.

3. In the Virginia colony, the _____ educated the children.

4. Plantation owners cultivated the cash crop of _____. Slaves from _____ did most of the work in the tobacco fields.

5. _____ servants worked for free to pay off their passage debt.

6. Members of the Virginia __Colony/__Company financed the establishment of the Virginia settlement.

7. German and Scotch-Irish settlers farmed the area (circle one) … of the Blue Ridge mountains.
    north   south   east   west

And One More for Fun!

Oops! Mom is not feeling well today. She asks you to hold the classes in your Virginia colony home classroom. It's time for some strategic planning so you can survive your day as teacher! Make a list of what you will teach below.

_____   _____

_____   _____

_____   _____

_____   _____

_____   _____

4.3c Money, banking, saving, and credit had various roles in colonial Virginia.

Money's Role in the Virginia Colony

Economic factors influenced life in the Virginia colony.

economy: the system of the use of money in society

Today, we generally use money to buy what we want or need. But few people in the Virginia colony had currency to buy goods and services. Because they did not have any money, they *bartered* with one another.

Barter was commonly used among the colonists to obtain the things that they needed or wanted. To barter is to trade or swap one thing for another. For example, a colonist who had extra corn might trade it for some fresh eggs from a colonist who owned a hen. Tobacco was a highly valued barter item. It was often used instead of money.

Circle the items below which might serve as something you could barter with another colonist.

Jelly

Apples

Tobacco

Garden Tools

Eggs

Cat

Butter Churn

Horse

Circle the services for which you might barter some of the goods previously pictured.

Lawn service

Dental work

Carpentry

Tow your car

A haircut

Blacksmithing

Pottery

Your Credit is Good Here!

consumer: a user of goods or services

Consumers could buy goods from merchants and shopkeepers on credit. They would pay their debts when the crops that they had grown were harvested.

A debt is something that you owe to someone else. Credit is getting something today that you promise you will pay for later.

Let's Shop!

It has been a busy morning on the farm. Your father is busy repairing tools. Your mother is busy preparing dinner. They send you to barter with merchants and shopkeepers for some things that they need. They give you a basket of fresh vegetables, a handmade blanket, and a fresh-baked pie. They also give you a list of items that they need: a pair of shoes for your little brother, some cornmeal, and nails.

Match the item that you would barter with the good that you receive in exchange.

Import and Export

Colonists exported natural resources. This means that they sold them to other countries. The colonists imported manufactured goods from England. This means that they received some of the things they needed for daily life from another country.

Between using barter and credit, and importing and exporting, the colonists managed to survive economically without actually having very much money. There were no banks in colonial Virginia.

Today we do not barter as much as colonists did. We pay cash for items we want or need. Or, we put our money in banks and write checks for goods and services. We may use credit cards to buy on credit. We may borrow money from a bank and go into debt. And we may put our money into the bank in order to save for what we may want to purchase later.

Everyone Was Part of the Economy!

Many types of people lived in the colony of Virginia. Some were wealthy plantation owners. These families enjoyed lives of luxury. However, everyone was expected to make some contribution. Even the aristocratic women spent hours doing fancy needlework. Young girls were taught these finer arts and crafts. Young boys learned plantation management at their father's side. Some of these fortunate people were the ones who established the first towns, colleges, churches, and other social institutions that helped the colony grow stronger. Some even established banks later in Virginia's history.

Other kinds of workers made their contribution to the needs of a growing society. While plantation owners generally grew tobacco, other farmers grew food crops such as wheat and corn. Artisans brought their skills with them to the colony and handcrafted fine silver or pewter dishes, tankards, and silverware. Skilled craftspeople made clothing, hats, shoes, saddles, and other goods people wanted or needed for daily life.

Other workers, such as ministers and doctors, provided services that the colonists wanted and needed. Some people ran inns or taverns; others opened shops. Less-skilled workers did menial, but necessary, work such as cleaning and hauling. No matter what their economic level, most of these colonists hoped to make more money so that they could improve the lives of their families.

Indentured servants and slaves worked hard at their jobs in the fields. However, they did not have the same motivation as those who were rewarded for hard work. Their goal was to work off their debt, or, in the case of slaves, just to survive until, perhaps, some turn of fate would offer them an opportunity for freedom.

1. Which do you think was most convenient in colonial Virginia?:
   __Money __Barter

2. Which do you think is most convenient today?:
   __Barter __Money

A Quick Review for YOU!

1. Few people in colonial Virginia used _____ to buy goods and services.
2. Instead of money, people would _____ with one another.
3. A valuable barter item was _____.
4. Consumers bought goods from shops on _____.
5. They would pay their _____ when the crops came in.

6. Colonists ☐ imported ☐ exported   natural resources.
7. Colonists ☐ imported ☐ exported   manufactured goods.

8. There were many banks in colonial Virginia. ☐ True or ☐ False?

And One More for Fun!

You saw a hoop-and-stick toy in the shop window. You really want it. You do not have any money. However, it is only two weeks before your farm's corn is harvested.

Below, write what you will say to the shopkeeper to try to convince him to let you have the toy on credit.

_____
_____
_____

4.3d - One of the most dramatic and historical events in Virginia was the American Revolution!

Conflict Was Bound to Happen

As Virginia and the other colonies continued to grow and prosper, conflicts developed between the colonies and Great Britain (England, Scotland, and Wales). They disagreed over many things. These conflicts eventually led the colonists to fight for freedom from their mother country. This war for independence is known as the American Revolution.

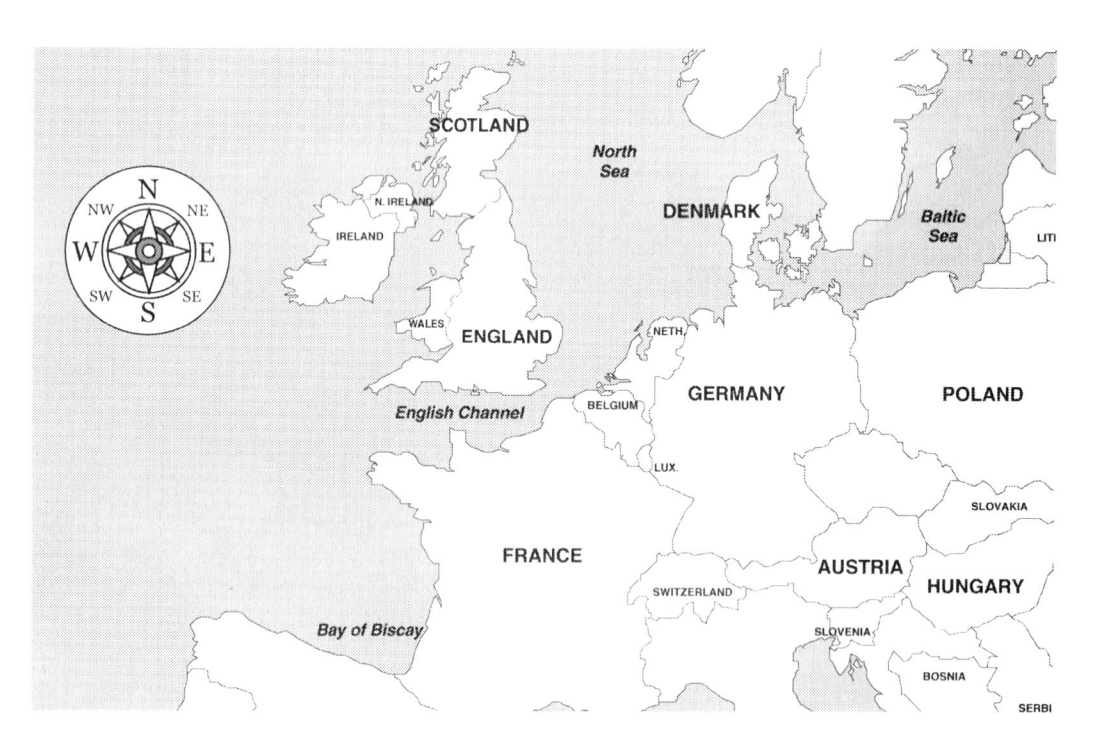

On the map above, circle the names of the places that make up the nation of Great Britain.

revolution: the overthrow of the government in authority

A Long List of Complaints

There were many conflicts between the colonies and Great Britain.

• The colonists and Great Britain disagreed over how to finance the French and Indian War.

• Conflict developed over the source of political authority. The colonists favored local assemblies as opposed to rule by Parliament.

• The colonists objected to taxation by England without representation.

Add the name of the missing colony.

The United States circa 1787.

Let's Take a Poll!

**Pretend you are a colonist.
You are asked your opinion about the following matters.
Put a checkmark to indicate how you feel.**

Hey, Colonists! Do we want to:

1. Pay tax, but have no say-so?	__YES __NO
2. Pay more than our fair share for war debt?	__YES __NO
3. Be ruled by faraway England?	__YES __NO
4. Establish local assemblies in the colonies?	__YES __NO
5. Fight for our independence?	__YES __NO

Conflict Leads to War!

Virginians played an active role in the colonies' struggle for independence. They participated in the events that led to war with England. Here are some of the ways that Virginians and other colonists responded to the growing conflict with Great Britain:

boycott: to not buy something as a way to protest

- Boycotted British goods

- Formed Committees of Correspondence

militia: an army made up of ordinary citizens

- Participated in Continental Congresses

- Joined militias

- Organized the Virginia Convention

- Appointed Thomas Jefferson to write the Declaration of Independence

All these activities helped put England on notice that the colonies would no longer go along with decisions being made for them. Virginians and other colonists made it clear that they wanted to be independent and make their own laws to live by. Participating in these events also helped to organize the colonists and to prepare them for the war that was to come.

Virginians and other colonists protested against unfair British rule and organized themselves for independence in many ways.

Circle the things that Virginians did to accomplish these things.

Thomas Jefferson was a Virginian who served in the House of Burgesses, as his father had before him. Jefferson's father died when he was only 14 years old, leaving him to run a large farm with 30 slaves. In 1760 he enrolled at the College of William and Mary in Williamsburg, from which he graduated two years later at the age of 19. After getting his degree, he studied law and was admitted to the bar in 1767. His great skill was in the written word. Other burgesses often asked Thomas Jefferson to write laws and resolutions for them. Then he was asked to write America's Declaration of Independence!

The American Revolution!

Virginians played an important role in the colonies' struggle for independence from Great Britain. During the Revolutionary War, Virginians made many contributions.

• Virginians fought the British from the Battle of Great Bridge to the siege of Yorktown
• Virginia provided food, clothing, and supplies for the Continental Army
• Virginia women took over the farming chores and supported troops in other ways

siege: an attack on a city or town by an army

Draw a circle around two of the places where Virginians fought during the Revolutionary War.

Number each scene to show the order in which events related to the American Revolution took place.

A. Pleading for representation

B. "We shall declare independence!"

C. The battle for freedom!

D. At peace in the colony

African-Americans and the Revolutionary War

African-Americans living in Virginia and the other colonies were divided in their feelings about the Revolutionary War. Some fought for the British because the British had promised them their freedom. Others wanted the colonists to win. One black man, James Lafayette, spied on the British to get information that would help the colonists win the war.

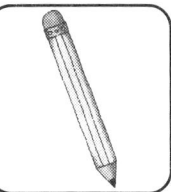

You have been a slave on a colonial plantation for many years. Now that the war with England has finally come, you must decide which side to fight for. Write your feelings here.

Timeline Activity:

Number these events in the order in which they happened:

- The Revolutionary War begins
- The Declaration of Independence is written
- Freedom! Welcome to the United States!
- Colonists say: "No taxation without representation!"

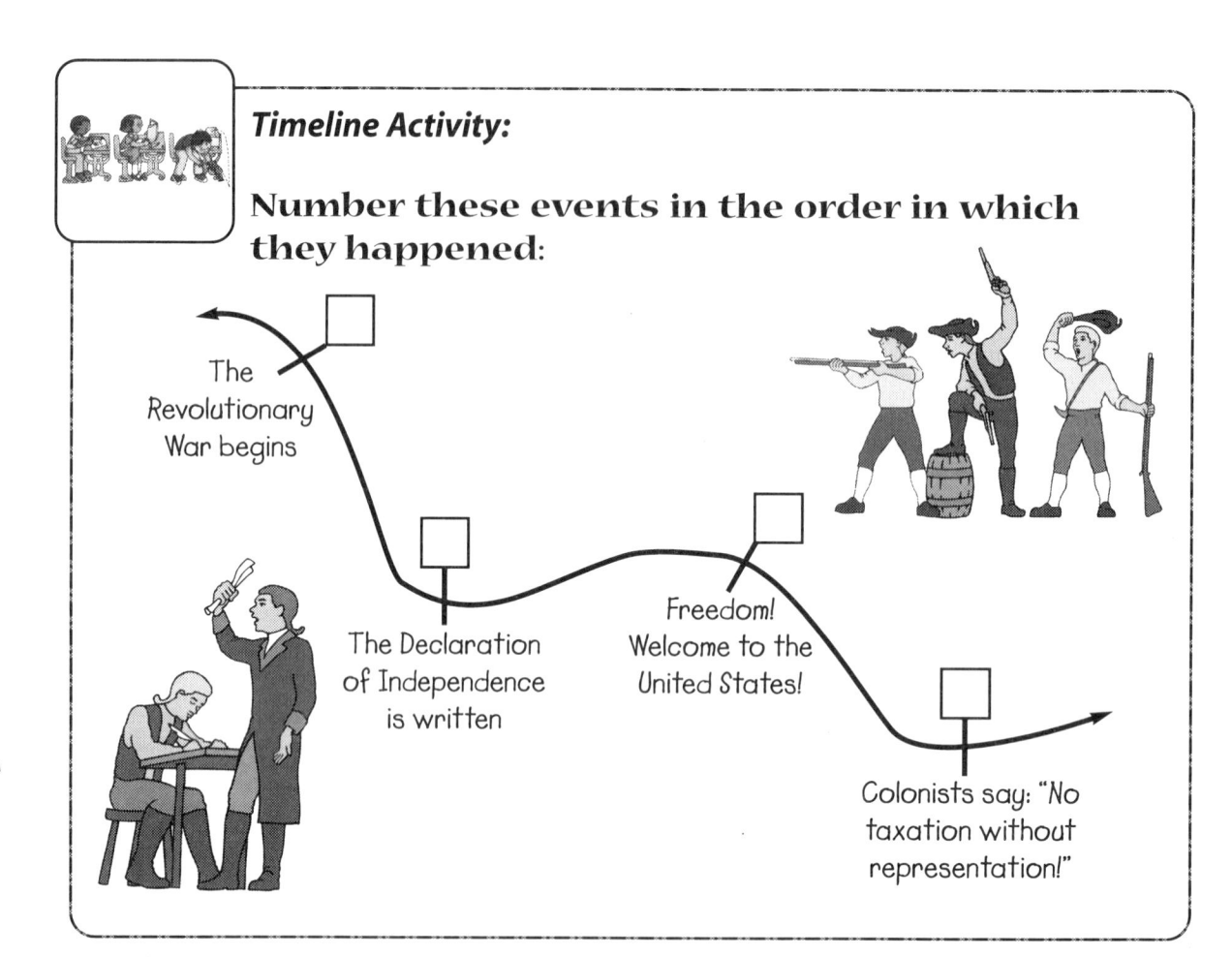

A Quick Review for YOU!

1. Virginians and other colonists did not want to pay _____ to Great Britain.

2. The colonists wanted to:
    A. Form local assemblies to govern themselves
    B. Be governed by Parliament

3. Thomas Jefferson was appointed to write the Declaration of _____.

4. During the Revolutionary War, Virginia women:
   A. fought   B. farmed   C. fled

5. African-Americans were _____ about the Revolutionary War.

And One More for Fun!

Match the words on the left with those on the right.

1. boycott   A. Convention

2. Committees of   B. British goods

3. Continental   C. Independence

4. Virginia   D. Correspondence

5. Declaration of   E. Congress

4.3e - Many prominent Virginians had the background and motivation to make significant contributions during the Revolutionary era.

They Called Them the Founding Fathers for a Good Reason!

Virginia's leaders played an important role in the founding of the United States. In fact, Virginians played the largest role of all the citizens of the original colonies in the founding of the United States! Let's take a look at some of these important Virginians:

• **George Washington** served as Commander-in-Chief of the Continental Army, President of the Constitutional Convention, and first President of the United States. He is known as the "Father of Our Country."

"I was born in Westmoreland County, Virginia, in 1732. At age 27, I became a member of the House of Burgesses. I was a delegate to the Continental Congresses in 1774 and 1775, and president of the Constitutional Convention in 1787. In 1789, I was elected—unanimously—as the first president of the United States of America. Pardon me, please, for not introducing myself. I am GEORGE WASHINGTON."

1. The word unanimous means:
A. in anger   B. in complete agreement   C. first

• **George Wythe** signed the Declaration of Independence and attended the Constitutional Convention of 1787.

"I was the first law professor in the United States, at the College of William and Mary from 1779-1789. I was born in Elizabeth City County, Virginia. My name is GEORGE WYTHE."

2. A convention is:
A. a formal meeting or assembly of delegates   B. an informal gathering

- **Thomas Jefferson** wrote the Declaration of Independence and the Virginia Statute for Religious Freedom. He also founded the University of Virginia and served as the President of the United States.

"Goochland (now Albemarle County), Virginia was my home. I was born there in 1743. I've been a lawyer, statesman, political theorist, musician, planter, architect, and archaeologist, and wrote the first draft of the Declaration of Independence. In 1801, I became America's third president. I enlarged America through the Louisiana Purchase, and sent Meriwether Lewis and William Clark on their famous expedition. However, I guess I'm most proud of founding the University of Virginia. An education is essential, you know. My name is THOMAS JEFFERSON."

1. The Declaration of Independence stated that the people wanted:

A. to go back home to England   B. to stop fighting   C. freedom

- **James Madison** was called the "Father of the Constitution." He also was a President of the United States.

"I was born in Port Conway, Virginia in 1751. I was a delegate to the Constitutional Convention and helped draft Virginia's constitution. I was honored by being called the "Father of the Constitution," even though I was only 25 years old when it was signed. I played a big role in creating the Bill of Rights. In 1801, I became U.S. Secretary of State, and from 1809-1817, I served as America's fourth president. My name is JAMES MADISON."

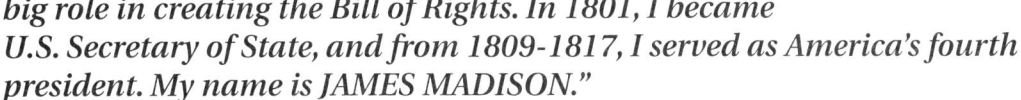

2. The Bill of Rights gave Americans:

A. Freedom of speech   B. Right to assemble
C. Freedom of the press   D. A, B, and C

- **James Monroe** was sent to France by Thomas Jefferson to negotiate for the Louisiana Territory. He also served as President of the United States.

"How could I have known, as a Westmoreland County, Virginia, baby in 1758, what a busy life I would have? I was a lawyer and statesman, and when I was age 25, a member of the Continental Congress. In 1817, I became America's fifth president. After that, did I retire? No way! I served as a U.S. senator, then minister to France, governor of Virginia, U.S. Secretary of State, and I was the author of the Monroe Doctrine. It was named after me. I'm JAMES MONROE."

The Louisiana Purchase

In 1803, a large tract of land was bought from France. This purchase almost doubled the size of the United States! This expanse of land extended roughly from the Mississippi River to the Rocky Mountains and from New Orleans, Louisiana to the Canadian border. This acquisition changed America from a small nation to a large one overnight. As colonists moved into the new territory, they were drawn westward even past the Rockies, all the way to the Pacific Ocean!

- **Patrick Henry** spoke out against taxation without representation. He said, "Give me liberty or give me death."

"I was born in 1736, became a member of the House of Burgesses and Continental Congresses, was a Virginia governor, and a leader in adding the Bill of Rights to the U.S. Constitution. My name is PATRICK HENRY."

1. Patrick Henry is best known as a:
A. writer   B. speaker   C. patriot   D. B and C

- **George Mason** wrote the Virginia Declaration of Rights, which is the basis for the U.S. Bill of Rights.

"I preferred to work behind the scenes instead of in public office. I wrote Virginia's Declaration of Rights. My name is GEORGE MASON."

2. The basis for the United States Bill of Rights was:
A. the United States Constitution
B. the Virginia Declaration of Rights
C. the Declaration of Independence

How did good writing and speaking skills help early Virginia leaders achieve their goals?

Write your ideas here:

What Were Their Motivations?

What did these Virginians hope to accomplish? At first, these men hoped to persuade Parliament to change the tax and trade laws and to treat colonists as equals. If the colonists were not going to be allowed to be represented in Parliament, then these men believed that the colonies should at least be able to make their own laws.

When it appeared that the colonies and England would not be able to come to an agreement, these Virginians helped the colonies act as independent states. In the meantime, they began to write documents that would limit the government's power to control private citizens.

The documents that they wrote still help us to govern America today!

Number the events below in the order that they happened during the Revolutionary era.

Washington crosses the Delaware to fight the British

Patrick Henry says... Give me LIBERTY... or give me DEATH!

Thomas Jefferson writes the Declaration of Independence

George Washington is sworn in as our first president

From the information in this chapter, make a list of 3 documents which early Virginia leaders wrote to help America achieve and maintain freedom.

_____
_____
_____

A Quick Review for YOU!

Match the people on the left with the fact about them on the right.

1. George Washington
2. Thomas Jefferson
3. James Madison
4. James Monroe
5. Patrick Henry

A. Said, "Give me liberty or give me death."
B. "Father of Our Country"
C. Wrote the Declaration of Independence
D. "Father of the Constitution"
E. Negotiated for the Louisiana Purchase

There's one thing about our founding fathers. They weren't ones to say, "I can't."

If you had been in Virginia during this revolutionary era when the nation was being formed, what would you have agreed to give a try?

- ❏ Write a long, important document
- ❏ Serve as president
- ❏ Be in charge of the army
- ❏ Attend a convention
- ❏ Make a speech
- ❏ Negotiate the purchase of land

4.3f - A number of important documents were written by early Virginia leaders which established many of the freedoms we still enjoy today!

Documents Do the Job!

When people feel very strongly about something, they try to find a clear way to express their feelings and ideas. One of the most useful and effective ways to do this is through a written document.

Early Virginians and Americans were eager to put their ideas about freedom into writing. They did this through four important documents:

- The Charters of the Virginia Company of London
- The Virginia Declaration of Rights
- The Virginia Statute for Religious Freedom
- The Declaration of Independence

These documents established the basic freedoms for Virginians and Americans. Let's look at each of these important documents individually.

Charters of the Virginia Company of London
These documents:
- Authorized the establishment of colonies
- Allowed for a representative form of government
- Extended English rights to the colonists

charter: a document issued by a government authority

amendment: a correction, improvement, or revision

Virginia Declaration of Rights
As a part of the Virginia Constitution, this document formed the basis of the Bill of Rights. The Bill of Rights is the first ten amendments to the U.S. Constitution.

Virginia Statute for Religious Freedom
This document:
- Separated church and state and established religious freedom
- Was the basis for the first amendment to the U.S. Constitution, which guarantees freedom of religion

guarantee: to promise, assure, or pledge

Declaration of Independence
This famous and important document was adopted July 4, 1776. It:
- Listed the basic rights of individuals
- Explained why the colonies should break away from England

Each of the four documents shown here was significant in establishing the rights of Virginians and Americans.

Match the document to one of the things it accomplished.

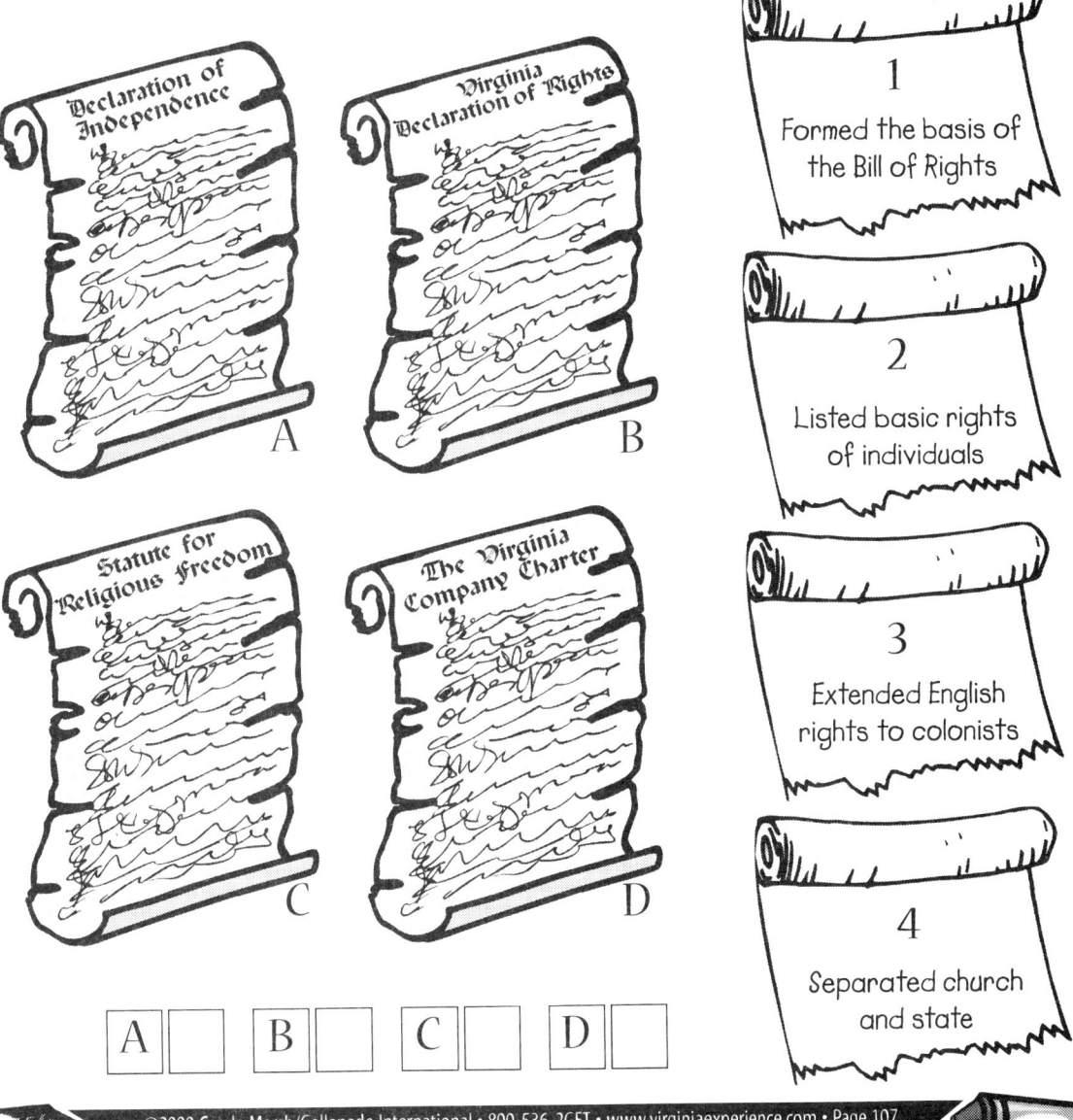

A. Declaration of Independence
B. Virginia Declaration of Rights
C. Statute for Religious Freedom
D. The Virginia Company Charter

1. Formed the basis of the Bill of Rights
2. Listed basic rights of individuals
3. Extended English rights to colonists
4. Separated church and state

A ☐ B ☐ C ☐ D ☐

You, a Virginia colonist, are trying to explain to someone from England why you think that the colonies should break away from England and form their own country. They are having difficulty understanding what you hope to achieve by this drastic action.

Explain the rights you expect to gain as clearly as you can.

_____
_____
_____
_____
_____

A Quick Review for YOU!

Match the document on the left with the fact about it on the right.

A. Declaration of Independence

B. Virginia Declaration of Rights

C. Virginia Statute for Religious Freedom

D. Charters of the Virginia Company of London

1. Authorized the establishment of the colonies

2. Was adopted July 4, 1776

3. Was part of the Virginia Constitution

4. Was the basis for the first amendment, guaranteeing religious freedom

Here We Go Again!

You, a Virginia colonist, are in a great debate with your English friend. She just cannot understand why you no longer want to be part of England. Put a V by your comments. Put an E by the comments she made.

☐ "I want the right to worship the way in which I choose, not the way some government tells me I will."

☐ "You are represented in your government, and I want the same privilege—especially if I have to pay taxes to that government."

☐ "My country established the Virginia colony and you are under English rule."

☐ "England can govern the colonies; it doesn't matter that we're all the way across the Atlantic Ocean from you."

☐ "Our Declaration of Independence will take care of this matter."

Here are some books about life in colonial America for you to enjoy!

Johnny Tremain, by Esther Forbes

The "Felicity" Series, by Valerie Tripp

Book of the American Colonies, by Howard Egger-Bovet and Marlene Smith-Baranzini; part of the Brown Paper School US Kids History Series

~ This book is not reproducible. ~

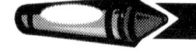

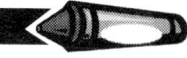

Chapter 2

George Washington was the first man to sign the U.S. Constitution as presiding officer of the 1787 Constitutional Convention in Philadelphia.

4.4a - Virginians made major contributions to the establishment of the U.S. Constitution, the Bill of Rights, and the success of the new national government.

Virginians Have the Best Ideas!

The ideas of Virginians were the basis for the principles of the new government of the United States. In fact, Virginians were the most important participants in the establishment of the new government. Here are some of the contributions Virginians made which helped get the new nation off on the right foot:

• Virginians participated in the Constitutional Convention of 1787.

• George Washington was president of the Constitutional Convention.

• James Madison's skills at compromise helped bring differing ideas together. This earned him the title of "Father of the Constitution."

compromise: to settle differences by each side giving up something to the other side

• The Bill of Rights was based on the Virginia Declaration of Rights, written by George Mason.

• The First Amendment to the U.S. Constitution guaranteed freedom of religion. This amendment was based on the Virginia Statute for Religious Freedom, written by Thomas Jefferson.

Answer the following questions:

1. Perhaps serving as president of the Constitutional Convention gave George Washington some experience in leadership he could use when he later became president of:

    A. The Constitution   B. The United States
    C. The Bill of Rights D. Virginia Statute for Religious Freedom

2. James Madison accomplished his goals through:

A. argument   B. belittling   C. compromise   D. debate

3. He was the "Father of the Constitution":

    A. George Washington   B. Thomas Jefferson
    C. George Mason   D. James Madison

Number which document came first in each pair below.

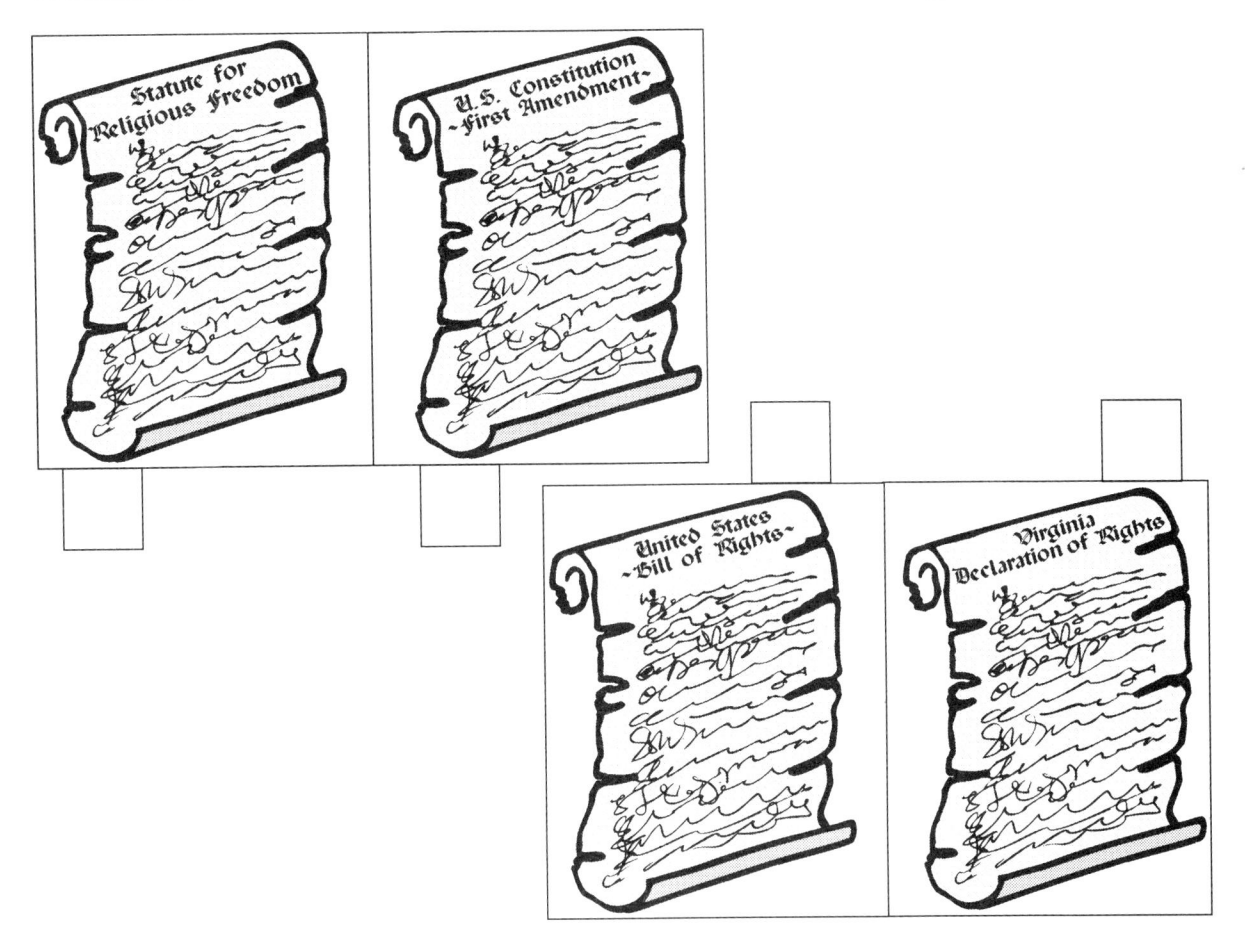

[Statute for Religious Freedom] [U.S. Constitution ~First Amendment~]

[United States ~Bill of Rights~] [Virginia Declaration of Rights]

Virginians Lead the New Nation to Success!

Virginians contributed to the successes of the new national government. Here are a few of the most famous Virginians to help the early government get off to a good start:

• George Washington served as the first President of the United States. He provided a model for future leaders.

• In fact, four of the first five U.S. Presidents were Virginians! These included George Washington, Thomas Jefferson, James Madison, and James Monroe. This is how Virginia got the title "Mother of Presidents."

• Thomas Jefferson authorized the purchase of the Louisiana Territory. This was known as the Louisiana Purchase.

• As U.S. President, James Monroe issued the Monroe Doctrine.

Match the people on the left with their contribution on the right:

A. George Washington

B. James Monroe

C. Thomas Jefferson

1. Wrote the Monroe Doctrine

2. Authorized the Louisiana Purchase

3. Served as the first U.S. President

model   compromise   freedom   ideas   principles

Fill in the blanks in the following paragraph from the word bank above.

1. The many important documents that early Virginians prepared formed the basis of the _____ of the new U.S. government.

2. To get the U.S. Constitution written, required _____ by all parties to bring their different _____ together.

3. Early Virginia leaders were interested in protecting religious _____.

4. As the first U.S. President, George Washington served as a _____ for future leaders.

A Quick Review for YOU!

1. Virginia has the title "Mother of …

    A. Freedom." B. Presidents."
    C. Religion." D. The Constitution."

2. The most important participants in the establishment of the new U.S. government were from:

    A. Louisiana   B. England   C. Virginia

3. The First Amendment to the U.S. Constitution gave Americans freedom of:

    A. speech   B. assembly
    C. religion   D. compromise

4. The Bill of Rights is based on the:

    A. Virginia Declaration of Rights   B. U.S. Constitution
    C. Louisiana Purchase   D. Monroe Doctrine
    E. Virginia Statute for Religious Freedom

5. How many of the first five U.S. Presidents were from Virginia?:

    A. 1   B. 2   C. 3   D. 4

Pretend you are a participant in the Constitutional Convention of 1787! There seem to be a lot of differing ideas. You know it will take a lot of compromise to get everyone to agree enough to get the Constitution written. James Madison asks your advice. Write what you tell him here!

4.4b - *Conflicts between northern and southern states, and within Virginia, led to secession.*

Conflict Leads to Crisis!

After the Revolutionary War, conflicts arose between the northern and southern states over states' rights and slavery. These same conflicts occurred within Virginia.

The North and the South had different economies:
- The economy in the northern part of the United States was industrialized.
- The economy in the southern part of the United States was agricultural and relied on slave labor.

A

B

Circle your answer:

1. Which scene represents the economy of the North at the time of the Civil War?:
   A or B

2. Which scene represents the basis of the economy in the southern states at the time of the Civil War?:
   A or B

The northern and southern states took different positions over the expansion of slavery into the new territories.

slave state: a state where the ownership of slaves is legal
free state: a state where the ownership of slaves is not legal

• Northern states wanted any new states to be "free states." Southern states wanted any new states to be "slave states."

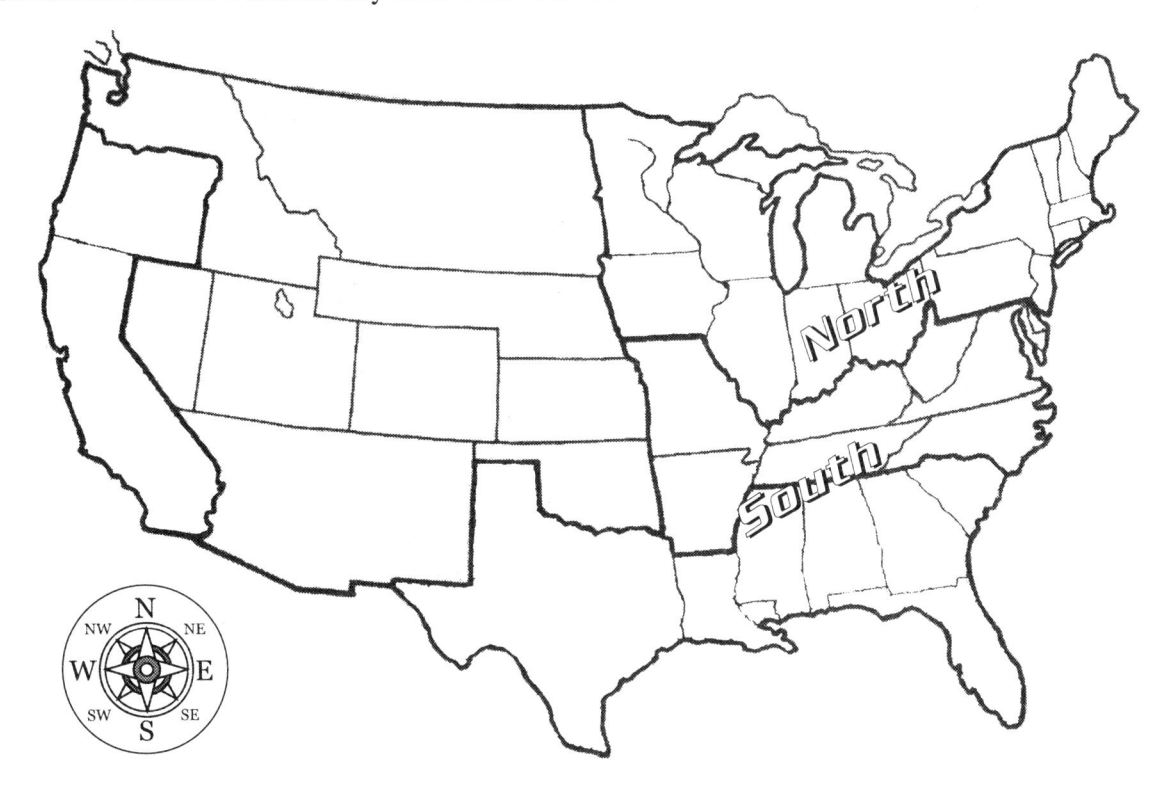

1. Which states on the map above were in favor of slavery and secession?:

    __North __South

2. Which states were in favor of abolition and preserving the Union?:

    __South __North

abolition: to do away with something; abolitionists wanted to do away with slavery

In Virginia, conflicts arose between the eastern counties that relied on slavery and the western counties that favored the abolition of slavery.

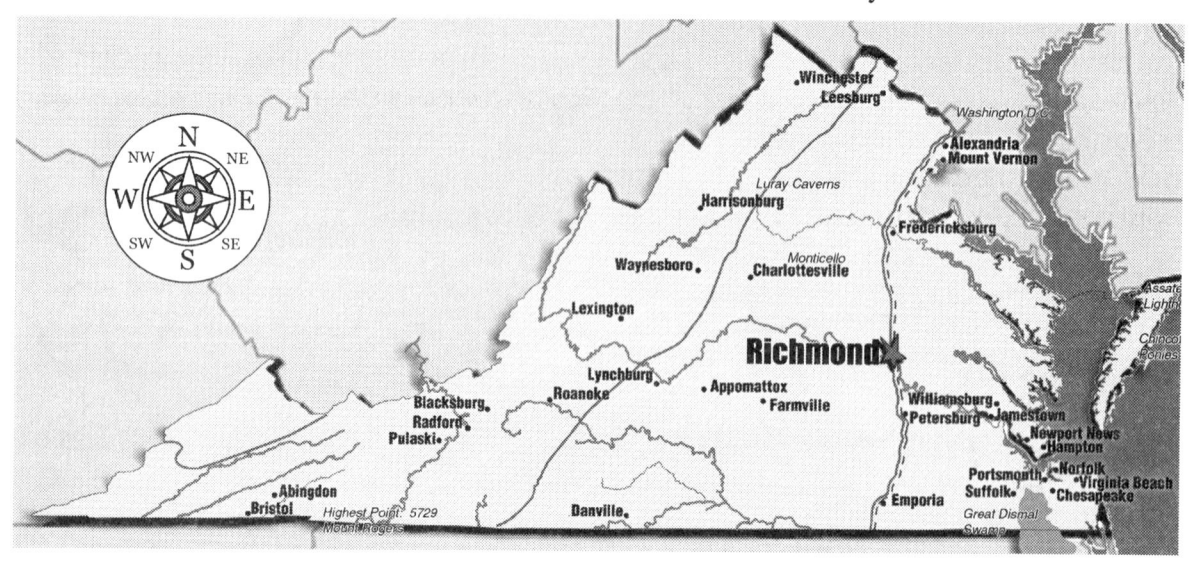

1. Which side of Virginia was in favor of slavery?: __East __West
2. Which side of Virginia was against slavery?: __West __East

The South Secedes! Virginia Secedes!

When the North and South were unable to resolve their conflicts, the South seceded from the United States.

secession: to pull away from; to leave

The Abolitionist Movement

Nat Turner and John Brown brought national attention to the abolitionist movement. Abolitionists wanted to see slaves go free.

John Brown seized the federal arsenal at Harpers Ferry. He hoped to arm slaves so that they could revolt.

Nat Turner led a revolt against plantation owners in Virginia. This was known as Nat Turner's Rebellion.

When President Abraham Lincoln called for troops to preserve the Union, Virginia seceded from the Union. The western counties of Virginia then broke away and formed a new state, West Virginia.

Number the events below in the order in which they occurred.

☐ Nat Turner leads rebellion   ☐ Virginia secedes from the Union   ☐ Southern states secede   ☐ West Virginia formed

The Civil War

Because the North and South could not resolve their conflicts, they fought one another in the Civil War. The issues that they were fighting over were:

- states' rights: the right of a state to decide for itself what it wants to do
- slavery
- the preservation of the Union

The Election of Lincoln

In 1860, Abraham Lincoln was elected president of the United States. Lincoln was against slavery. By the time he actually took office, seven southern states had already seceded from the Union. They not only wanted to preserve the institution of slavery, but also wanted the right to make their own laws without interference from the federal government.

These states formed a separate government. They called this government the Confederate States of America. Lincoln insisted that secession was illegal. He swore that he would protect federal possessions located in the South.

On April 12, 1861, Confederate soldiers tried to take Fort Sumter, a federal military fortification in the harbor of Charleston, South Carolina. Edmund Ruffin, a Virginian, fired the first shot! President Lincoln asked several states, including Virginia, to fight to hold the fort for the Union. Virginia refused. On April 14, Fort Sumter was forced to surrender. Virginia seceded from the Union on April 17 and joined the Confederacy on April 25. At that time, the capital of the Confederacy was moved from its original location in Montgomery, Alabama to Richmond, Virginia.

Match the cause with its effect:

1. North and South unable to agree
2. President Lincoln calls out troops
3. Western counties against slavery

A. West Virginia formed
B. Virginia and southern states secede
C. Civil War fought

A Quick Review for YOU!

1. Conflicts over slavery and other issues arose between:

    A. Northern and Southern states
    B. Eastern Virginia and western Virginia
    C. Both A and B
    D. Neither A nor B

2. A person in favor of freeing slaves was called a/an:

    A. secessionist   B. abolitionist   C. preservationist

3. The Civil War was fought over:

    A. slavery   B. states' rights   C. Union preservation
    D. A, B, and C

4. Slave states were found in the ___North ___South

5. Nat Turner and John Brown helped slaves:

    A. revolt   B. secede   C. form a new state

6. Virginia seceded from the United States: ___before ___after other southern states.

4.4c - Virginia played a major role in the Civil War. Many battles were fought in the state. Many Virginians became military leaders.

The Civil War in Virginia

Much of the Civil War was fought in Virginia. After Virginia seceded from the United States, the capital of the Confederacy was moved to Richmond, Virginia.

Many Civil War battles were fought in Virginia because of the location of Richmond, the capital of the Confederacy, and Washington, D.C., the capital of the United States.

The first battle of the Civil War was fought at Manassas, Virginia on Bull Run Creek. The Confederacy won this battle.

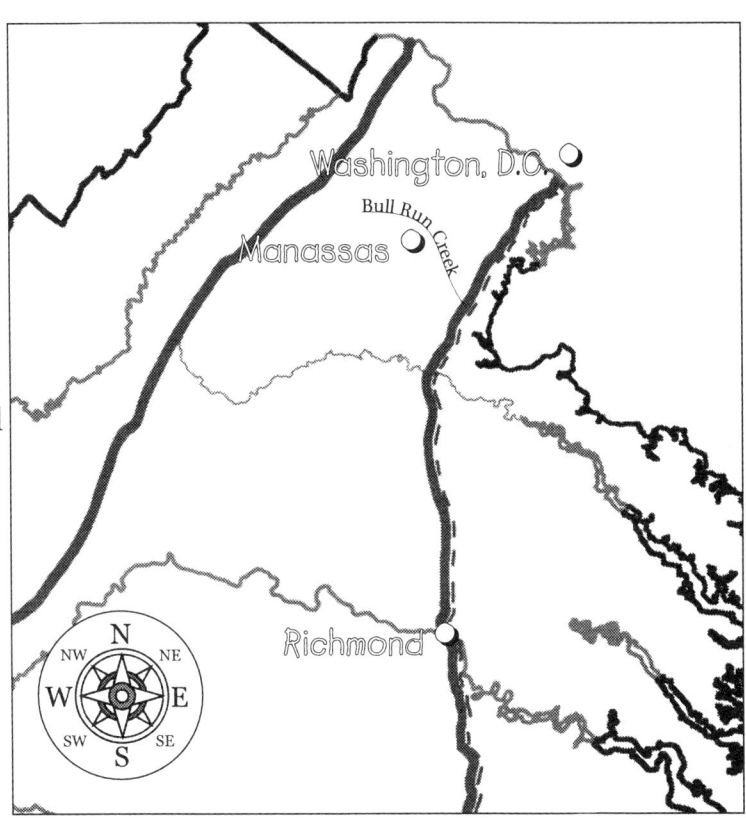

Answer the following questions:

1. Bull Run Creek is located near this Civil War battle site: _____

2. The capital of the Confederacy was in this Virginia city: _____

3. Washington, D.C. is the capital of:

    A. The Confederacy   B. The United States   C. The Civil War

Virginians Lead the Confederacy!

Many Virginians were leaders in the Confederate army.

Robert E. Lee:
• Commanded the Confederate Army during the Civil War
• He was offered command of the Union forces at the beginning of the Civil War, but he resigned rather than fight against his native state of Virginia.

resign: to give up or quit, as in to quit your job, or to give up a position of responsibility

J.E.B. Stuart:
• He also resigned from the United States Army to join the Confederate Army.
• Called the "eyes of the Army" by Robert E. Lee

Thomas "Stonewall" Jackson:
• A general in the Confederate Army
• Earned the nickname "Stonewall" at the Battle of Bull Run

The War Ends

The Civil War ended at Appomattox Court House, Virginia. It was here that General Robert E. Lee surrendered his army to Union General Ulysses S. Grant.

surrender: to give up, as in to give up to an enemy force

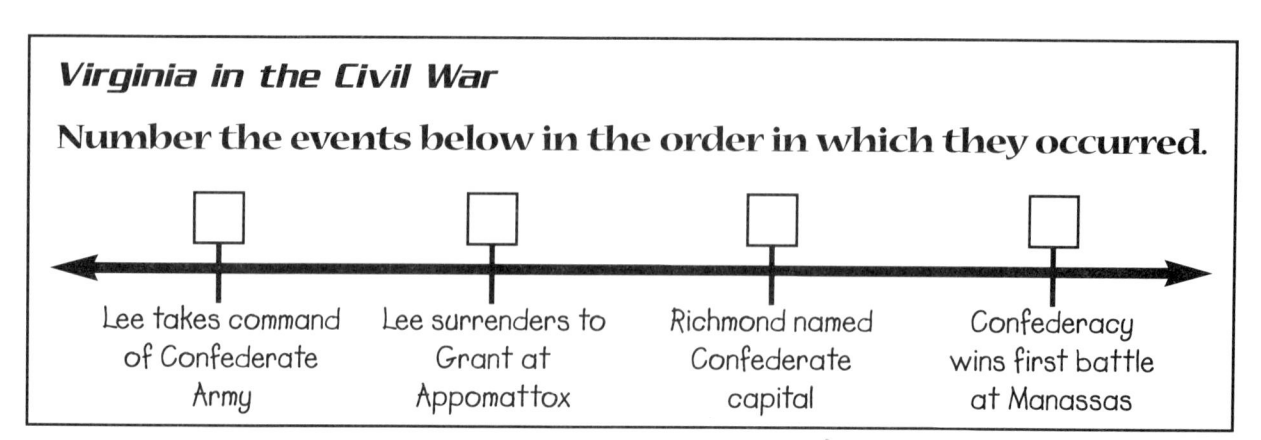

Virginia in the Civil War

Number the events below in the order in which they occurred.

Lee takes command of Confederate Army	Lee surrenders to Grant at Appomattox	Richmond named Confederate capital	Confederacy wins first battle at Manassas
☐	☐	☐	☐

Standing Like a Stone Wall!

Legend says that General Thomas Jackson was so steadfast in battle that he was compared to a "stone wall." That is how he got his nickname, "Stonewall."

Match the person on the left with their Civil War role on the right:

1. J.E.B. Stuart
2. Thomas "Stonewall" Jackson
3. Robert E. Lee

A. Served as the "eyes" of the Confederate Army
B. Commander of the Confederate Army
C. General at the Battle of Bull Run

In an encyclopedia, look up the Civil War.

1. When was the Battle of Bull Run fought?
   _____

2. On what date did the Civil War end at Appomattox Court House?
   _____

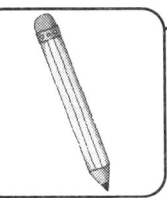

resign   surrender   command   battle

Use the words in the word bank above to fill in the blanks below.

1. I think I would _____ before I would fight against my own state.

2. It is hard to imagine what it was like during the _____ at Bull Run Creek near Manassas during the Civil War.

3. A general's job is to take _____ during a battle.

4. It must have been difficult for General Lee to _____ his army to General Grant.

A Quick Review for You!

1. The capital of the Confederacy was moved to Richmond __before __after Virginia seceded from the Union.

2. Much of the Civil War was fought in Virginia because:

     A. General Lee lived there   B. There were creeks and stone walls
     C. of the location of Richmond and Washington, D.C.

3. Who won the first battle of the Civil War?

     A. The Union Army   B. The Confederate Army

4. He was the "eyes of the Confederate Army."

     A. Thomas "Stonewall" Jackson   B. Robert E. Lee
     C. Ulysses S. Grant   D. J.E.B. Stuart

5. The Civil War ended at:

     A. Washington, D.C.   B. Appomattox Court House
     C. Richmond, Virginia   D. Manassas, Virginia

And One More for Fun!

You have been asked to serve as general of the Army of the planet Uh Oh. You pretty much agree with the people on planet Uh Oh, but there is one problem. They plan to attack your home planet of Skippy. You must choose: Fight against your home planet, or turn down the offer to be general. Make your choice and explain it here:

Chapter 3

The world's first successful electric railway was located in Richmond in 1888. It connected the suburbs with downtown, and became the model for cities all over the world.

*4.5a - The Reconstruction Period, which followed the Civil War,
was an especially difficult time for Virginians.*

Reconstruction — No Fun for Anyone!

The period following the end of the Civil War was called Reconstruction. Life was very difficult for Virginians during the Reconstruction Period. Virginians had to rebuild the state after the Civil War.

The problems that Virginians faced during the Reconstruction Period were social, political, and economic. These problems included:

- Newly freed slaves had little food, clothing, or shelter, and no way to make a living.

- The economy of Virginia had collapsed. Confederate money had no value.

- Railroads, bridges, and crops were destroyed during the Civil War.

- Virginia had no functioning government.

What Do We Do Now?

As you can see, Virginians had many problems to solve following the Civil War.

Match the problem below with the effect it had:

1. No government
2. Worthless money
3. Destroyed crops

A. Hunger and starvation
B. No one in charge
C. No way to buy anything

Virginians Rebuild!

As Virginians identified the many problems they had to solve, they began to come up with responses and solutions. Some of these were:

- The U.S. Congress created the Freedman's Bureau to help newly freed slaves cope with a lack of food, clothing, shelter, and jobs.

- Because plantation owners did not have money to pay workers, and because former slaves needed land and work, sharecropping developed. Sharecropping let freed blacks work the land in exchange for part of the harvest and, eventually, the ownership of their own piece of farmland.

- Virginia adopted a new state constitution which banned slavery and gave black men the right to vote.

- People moved from the countryside to cities in search of economic opportunities.

Answer the following questions:

1. The Freedman's Bureau was created to help:

    A. Congress
    C. plantation owners
    B. freed slaves
    D. bridge builders

2. What type of opportunity might a Virginian who moved to the city from the countryside during the Reconstruction Period have found?

    A. sharecropping   B. construction job   C. banker

3. Plantation owners used this method to help freed slaves get back to work:

    A. sharecropping   B. railroading   C. voting

4. Virginia's new state constitution:

   A. banned slavery and gave black men the vote
   B. forced people to move from the countryside to the city
   C. gave Confederate money value

5. As Virginians moved from the countryside to the cities, the population of cities:

   A. increased   B. decreased   C. stayed the same

The Civil War has just ended. You have been put in charge of making a plan to help freed slaves during this period of reconstruction.

What are some things you would do to help the freed slaves?

☐ Provide food

☐ Build a bridge

☐ Plan a party

☐ Build homes

☐ Provide clothing

☐ Plant crops

☐ Go swimming

A Quick Review for YOU!

1. The period following the Civil War was known as:

    A. Freedman
    B. Sharecropping
    C. Reconstruction

2. The Reconstruction Period came __before __after the Civil War.

3. One of Virginia's biggest **political** problems after the Civil War was that it had no:

    A. food, clothing, or shelter
    B. functioning government
    C. railroads or bridges

4. Confederate money was __worthless __valuable following the Civil War.

5. This banned slavery and gave black men the right to vote:

    A. The Freedman's Bureau
    B. The new state constitution
    C. Plantation owners

4.5b - Segregation and Jim Crow laws had an impact on Virginia life in the 20th century.

Segregation in Virginia

The practice of segregation had a significant impact on life in Virginia in the 20th century. **Segregation** meant that society in Virginia was segregated, or divided, by race. Because of this, African-Americans established their own churches, businesses, and schools. For example, Maggie Lena Walker, a black woman, opened the first bank for African-Americans.

A Bad Turn of Events

During the Reconstruction Period, African-Americans had begun to have some power in Virginia's government. However, these gains were reversed when laws were passed that made it difficult for African-Americans to vote and hold office. These laws imposed poll taxes and literacy tests. In other words, if blacks could not pay the poll tax or pass the literacy test, they were not allowed to vote or hold office.

Even though black families wanted to better themselves, segregation put up many barriers to any hope of success. In spite of their efforts, many whites continued to be prejudiced against blacks. Virginia, like most of the South, was divided along racial lines. It would take new laws and new ways of thinking to end segregation and prejudice.

Jim Crow Laws

Certain laws, called Jim Crow laws, discriminated against African-Americans in Virginia. These laws also reinforced prejudices held by white people about black people.

Under these Jim Crow laws, African-Americans were not allowed to:
- Ride in the same section of buses and trains as whites
- Eat in the same restaurants as whites
- Attend the same public schools as white citizens

These laws also had an impact on the economic life of African-Americans. For example, it was legal for an employer to pay blacks less money than white workers were paid.

Answer the following questions about segregation and Jim Crow laws.

1. An example of segregation is:

    A. Not being able to go to the bank
    B. Not being allowed to go to the same school as white children
    C. Not being able to travel to another state

2. Maggie Lena Walker opened the first one of these for African-Americans:

    A. restaurant   B. bus station
    C. bank   D. school

3. The result of Jim Crow laws and segregation was:

    A. discrimination   B. literacy   C. employment

4. A poll tax and literacy test often kept African-Americans from:

    A. eating   B. riding   C. voting

5. Under Jim Crow laws, white employers were legally allowed to pay African-Americans __ more __ less than they paid white workers.

6. Segregation divided black and white Virginians by:

    A. age   B. race   C. gender

How would you have felt...?

If you were not allowed to go to the same school as other children in your community?

If you did the same job but were paid less money?

If you could not eat at the same restaurant as other people?

If you were not allowed to vote because of your race?

Which of the following is an example of prejudice?:

A. "You can't play sports because you are a girl!"

B. "You are not as good as me because your skin is a different color!"

C. "You are too old to do that job!"

D. A, B, and C

*4.5c - From the Reconstruction Period to the 20th century,
Virginia had a transition to an urban society from a rural one.*

Leaving the Farms for the City!

Following the Reconstruction Period, Virginia changed from a rural, agricultural society to a more urban, industrial society.

1. Match the following:

1. rural
2. urban
3. agricultural
4. industrial

A. based on farming
B. city
C. based on technology
D. country

Because old systems of farming were no longer effective and crop prices were low, it became more difficult for farmers to make a living. Therefore, people began to move from the countryside to cities. This caused Virginia's cities to grow.

What were people looking for in the cities? They hoped to find economic opportunities, such as more and better jobs.

2. An example of an economic opportunity found in the city is:
A. a job with good pay and benefits
B. a company that will train you
C. a work/study program where you can earn money and improve your skills
D. A, B, and C

Virginia's Cities Grow!

Other factors also caused Virginia's cities to grow. These included technological developments in transportation, roads, railroads, and streetcars. Another reason for growth was coal mining, which caused people to move from the countryside to towns and cities to find jobs.

3. What caused Virginia's cities and towns to grow in the 20th century?
A. people moving to the city from the country
B. improved methods of farming
C. a lack of transportation

Match the cause on the left with its effect on the right.

___ 1. Freed slaves had no food, clothing, or housing.

___ 2. Plantation owners could not pay slaves.

___ 3. Slaves could not find work in the country.

A. Sharecropping developed.

B. The Freedman's Bureau was created.

C. Many freed slaves moved to the cities.

A Quick Review for YOU!

Answer the following questions:

1. Railroads and streetcars are examples of:
    A. technology   B. transportation   C. trips to town

2. You are more likely to find agricultural activities in this area:
    A. rural   B. city

3. You are more likely to find industry and technology in this area:
    A. countryside   B. town/city

4. Following Reconstruction, Virginia's farmers had ___more ___less economic opportunity.

And One More for Fun!

Wow! You have lived on the farm in a small town all your life. It seems like a big decision to move to a big city. What will you do? Where will you live? How will you get around? You write a letter to your city friend and ask her all these questions. This is what she writes back to you:

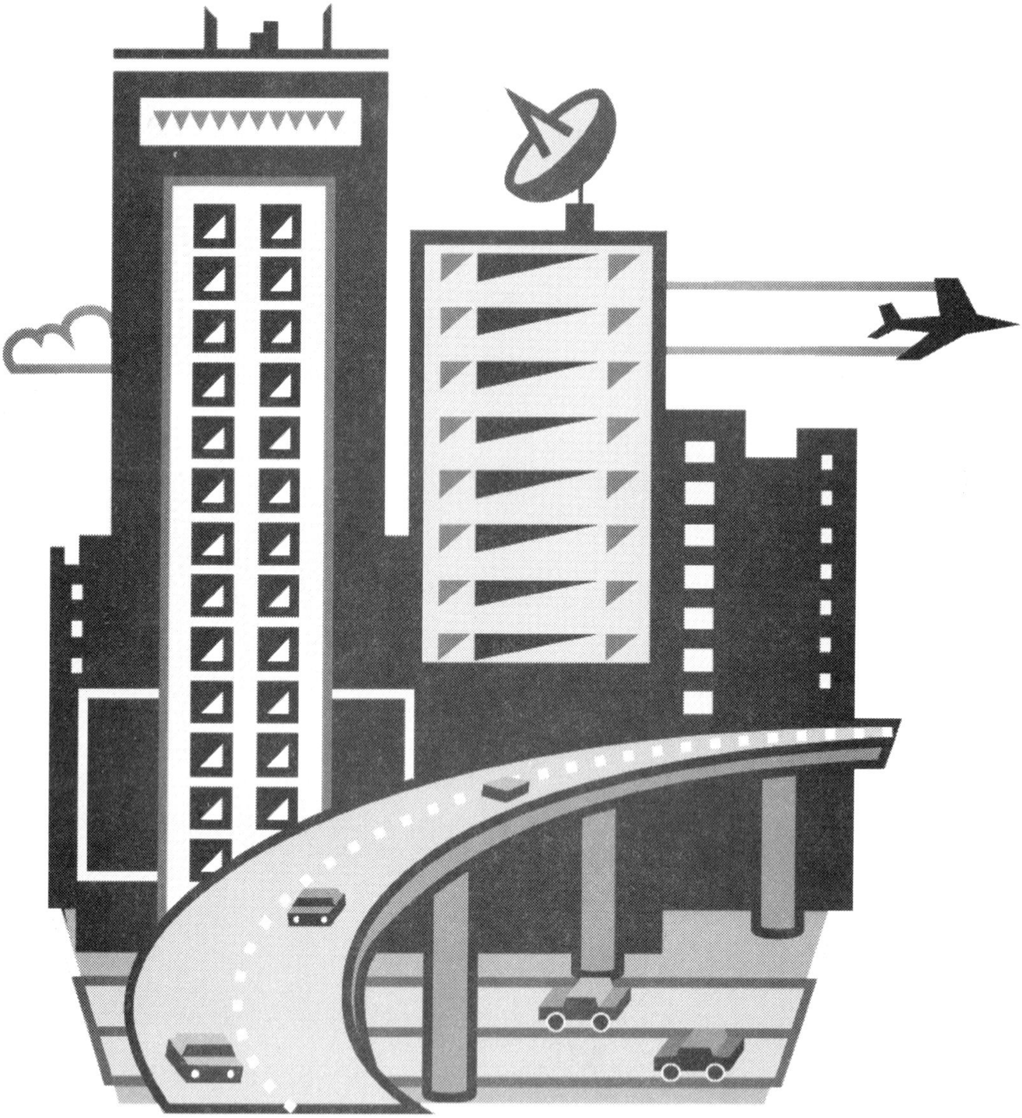

~ This book is not reproducible. ~

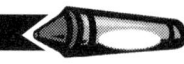

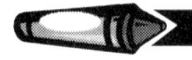

Chapter 4

Fifty percent of all Internet traffic passes through northern Virginia, where the headquarters of America Online are located. The Pentagon, also found in Virginia, is the world's largest office building. It covers 6.5 million square feet and was built in 16 months, completed in 1941.

4.6a - Many individuals contributed to the history of Virginia and the United States in the 20th century!

Accomplished Virginians!

A number of prominent Virginians made great contributions to the history of our state and to the nation during the 20th century. Let's look at just a few of the people who have had such an influence on our lives.

Woodrow Wilson was:
- born in Virginia
- 28th President of the United States.

•Harry F. Byrd, Sr.:
- served as governor of Virginia
- was a U.S. senator from Virginia
- known for his "pay as you go" policy to improve state roads
- led the Massive Resistance Movement against the integration of Virginia's public schools

"Pay as you go" was a policy of paying for road improvements as they were made, instead of the state going into debt for such construction. ***Massive Resistance*** was the attempt to avoid the integration of public schools in Virginia.

L. Douglas Wilder:
- Governor of Virginia
- First African-American governor in the United States

Arthur Ashe:
- Native of Richmond, Virginia
- World champion tennis player
- First African-American from Virginia to play professional tennis

Answer the following questions:

1. Integration came __before __after segregation.

2. "Pay as you go" was a __good __bad way to pay for road construction.

3. Massive Resistance was a __good __poor way to move from segregation to integration.

A Quick Review for YOU!

Match the person on the left with their accomplishment on the right:

1. Arthur Ashe
2. Woodrow Wilson
3. L. Douglas Wilder
4. Harry F. Byrd, Sr.

A. Virginia governor and senator
B. World tennis champion
C. First African-American governor in U.S.
D. 28th President of the U.S.

A great book about one young girl's struggle for equal rights is *Roll of Thunder, Hear My Cry*, by Mildred D. Taylor.

4.6b - In Virginia in the 20th century, social and political events were linked to desegregation and Massive Resistance.

The Civil Rights Movement in Virginia

During World War II, many African-Americans fought for their country. When the war was over, they returned home determined to obtain their full civil rights. This campaign for black rights is called the Civil Rights Movement. During the 20th century, Virginia struggled over the issue of civil rights.

1. Which came first?
A. The Civil Rights Movement
B. World War II

Civil rights are the privileges that you enjoy as a citizen. They can include the right to vote or an equal opportunity to get a job. For blacks during this era, it also meant being able to sit anywhere you wanted to on a bus or being served in any restaurant.

2. Fill in the Blank: Because they had fought for their _____, African-Americans believed they should have rights equal to those of whites.

In the 1950s and 1960s, African-Americans began to protest against segregation and unfair laws. Blacks in Virginia, like others across the South, began to participate in boycotts, sit-ins, and marches in order to make themselves heard and understood.

boycott: to not buy something as a way to protest

African-Americans wanted to eliminate *prejudice* against them. An example of prejudice is assuming that something is true that is actually false. If you say, "All blue-eyed people are silly," you are being prejudiced. This is an unfair statement, as well as an untrue one.

sit-in: to protest something by sitting in a place and refusing to move. African-Americans and others participated in boycotts and sit-ins during the Civil Rights Movement.

Blacks also fought *discrimination*. They did not believe that it was right for them to be discriminated against because of the color of their skin. For example, they did not believe that their race made any difference when it came to the jobs that they could do.

1. Check the statements you think are prejudiced:
___ A. A city person could never be a farmer.
___ B. A woman should not be a firefighter.
___ C. Someone in a wheelchair cannot be a writer.

What African-Americans wanted most of all was to be fully integrated into American society. Many Virginians resisted these changes. They did not like being challenged by blacks; they did not want change. They did not want to extend the civil rights that they enjoyed to African-Americans. They tried to get around this through:

- **Massive Resistance**: A movement to avoid integration and continue to enforce segregation

- **"Separate but equal"**: This policy tried to offer African-Americans their own schools where they would be treated "equally" but continue to be "separate" from whites.

In spite of boycotts and sit-ins by African-Americans, and widespread resistance to integration by whites, Virginia eventually achieved integration.

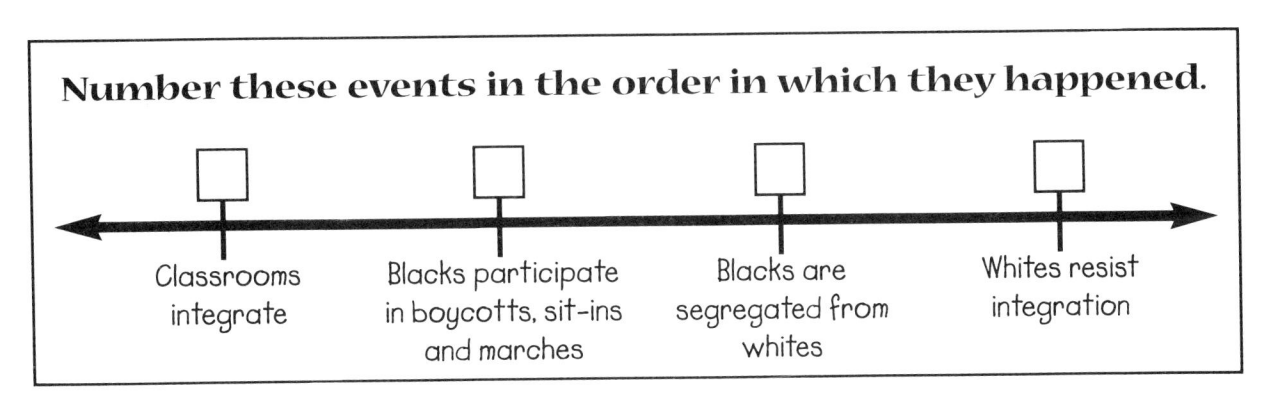

Number these events in the order in which they happened.

Classrooms integrate	Blacks participate in boycotts, sit-ins and marches	Blacks are segregated from whites	Whites resist integration
☐	☐	☐	☐

Cause and Effect

Match the situation on the left with its likely result on the right.

1. You defend your nation in war.

2. You work against new laws.

3. You boycott a store which has unfair hiring practices.

A. Hiring practices are improved.

B. You expect equal rights when you return home.

C. You find that the laws are upheld, in spite of your efforts to fight them.

A Quick Review for YOU!

1. The period of time when African-Americans and others worked to help blacks obtain equal treatment is known as the:

   A. Civil Rights Movement   B. World War II   C. Massive Resistance

2. African-Americans __did __did not want to be "separate but equal."

3. African-Americans and others protested prejudice and discrimination through:

   A. fighting a world war   B. boycotts and sit-ins   C. Massive Resistance

4.6c - Advances in transportation and communication in the 20th Century had a significant impact on Virginia.

Virginia On the Move!

In the 20th Century, Virginia saw many advances in transportation and communication. These advances facilitated migration and led to increased economic development.

migration: the movement from one place to another

Industries in Virginia produce goods and services used throughout the United States. Transportation-related improvements help move raw materials to manufacturing centers and finished products to markets. These improvements included:

- an extensive highway system across the state
- the expansion of railroads
- an increase in airports and airplanes

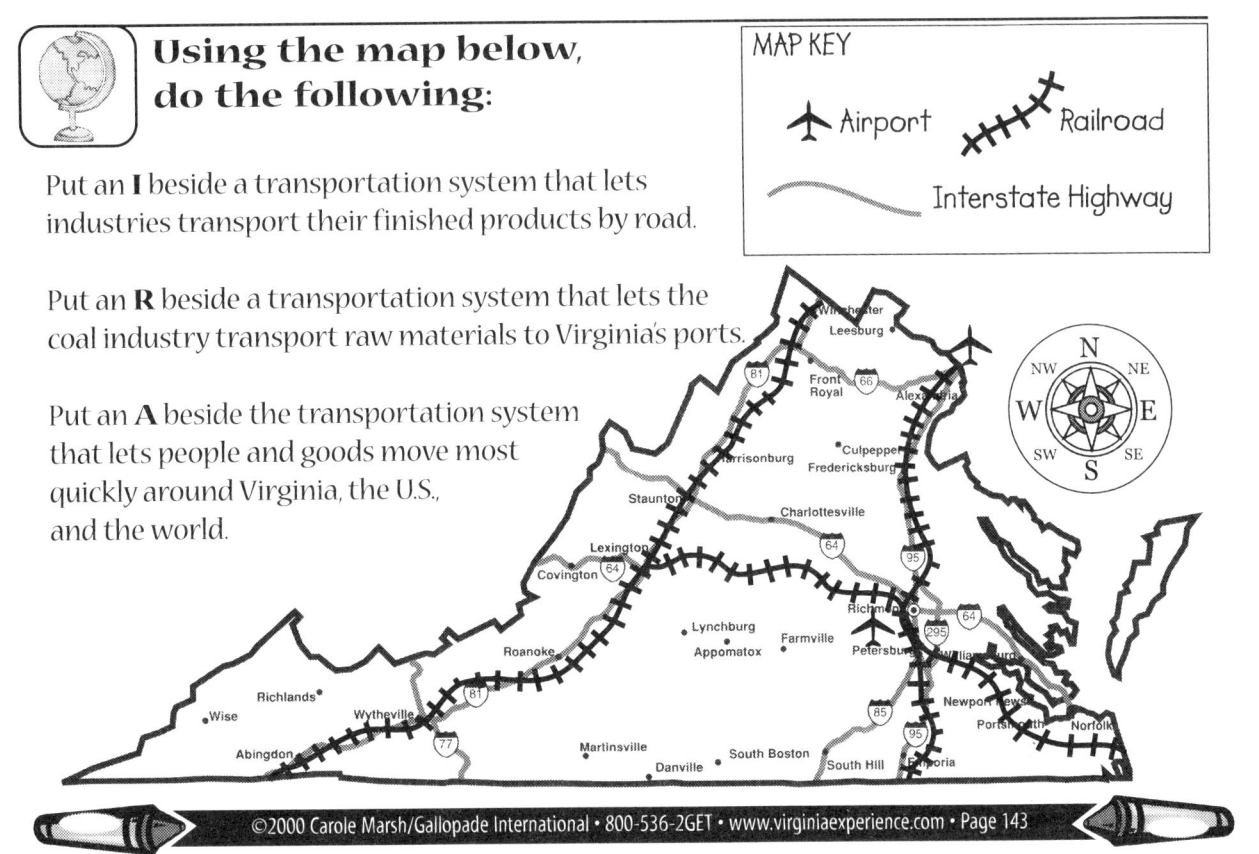

Using the map below, do the following:

Put an **I** beside a transportation system that lets industries transport their finished products by road.

Put an **R** beside a transportation system that lets the coal industry transport raw materials to Virginia's ports.

Put an **A** beside the transportation system that lets people and goods move most quickly around Virginia, the U.S., and the world.

MAP KEY
- Airport
- Railroad
- Interstate Highway

The Bigger Picture!

Virginia is an important part of the U.S. economy. Many people from other places in the United States and from around the world have migrated to Virginia for employment. They work in the state's many industries which produce goods and products. They also work in Virginia's service industries.

Some of the goods that Virginia exports include:

- textiles
- coal
- ships
- agricultural products, including tobacco and poultry

Services are things that people do for other people that they cannot, or do not want to, do for themselves. Examples of services include dry cleaning, package delivery, and computer repair. Tourism is one of Virginia's largest service industries and is a major part of the state's economy.

Check which people work in Virginia's tourism industry:

- ☐ Hotel/motel housekeeper
- ☐ Airline reservations clerk
- ☐ Travel agent
- ☐ Tour bus driver
- ☐ Historic site guide
- ☐ All of these

Advances in communication systems also helped Virginia achieve greater economic growth. Virginia has one of the greatest concentrations of high-technology industries in the United States.

Mega-what?!

Eastern Virginia is part of the northeast *megalopolis*. The northeast megalopolis is a string of urbanized areas extending along the Atlantic Coast from Boston south to the Hampton Roads area. Virginia became a part of this megalopolis because of its extensive economic development.

Draw a line from one end of the northeast megalopolis to the other, going through the major cities.
Draw a circle around the nation's capital.
Draw a star on the capital of Virginia.

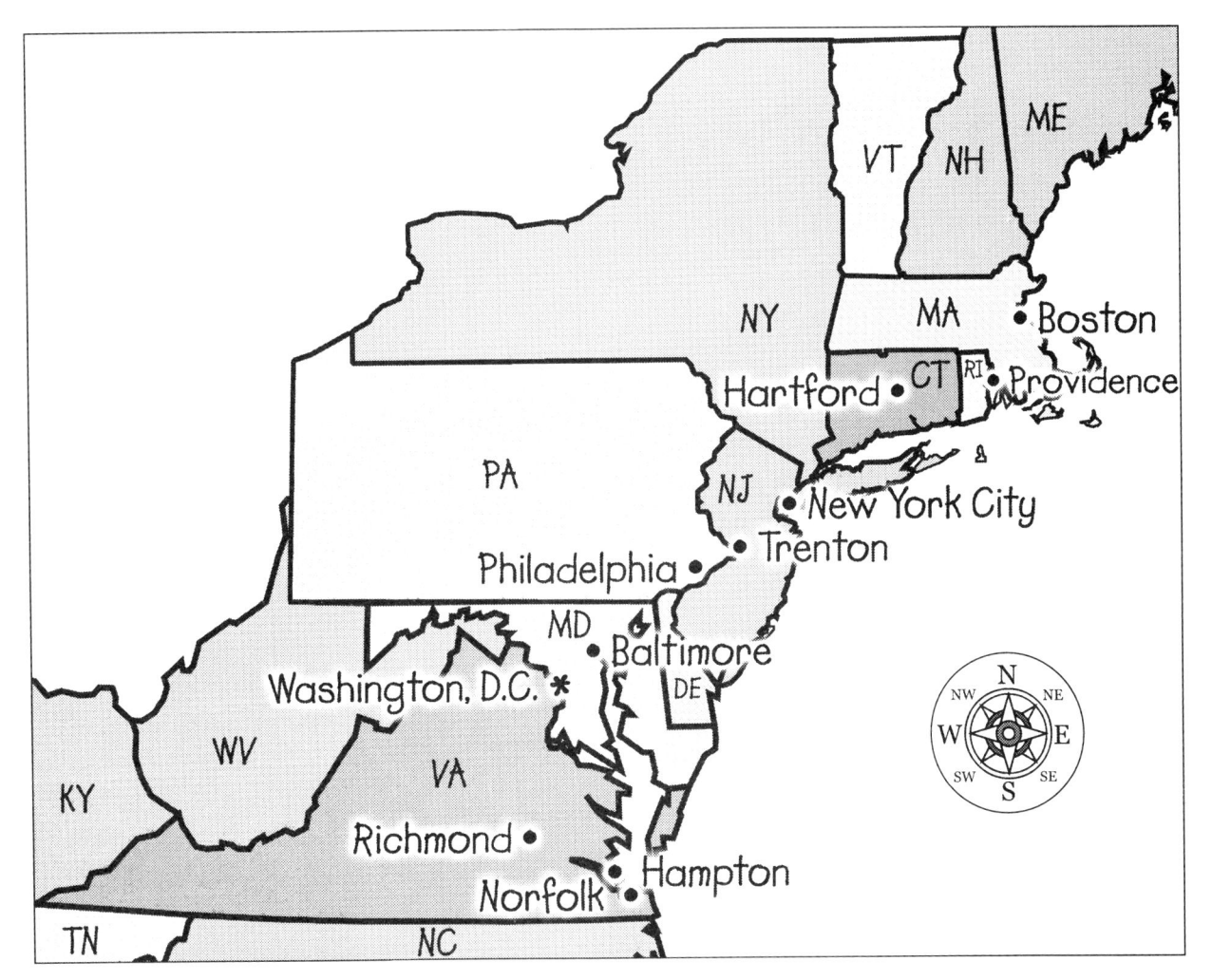

The federal government has a significant impact on Virginia's economy. Many Virginians are employed by the federal government in the Washington, D.C. metropolitan area. Federal military installations employ many people in the Hampton Roads area.

metropolitan: a city and its surrounding developed area

Northern Virginia has one of the largest concentrations of high-technology industries in the United States.

Can you identify these people and their jobs?

Put an **A** by the person involved in Virginia's shipbuilding industry.

Put a **B** by the people working at a military installation.

Put a **C** by the person working at a federal government office.

You have a friend who lives in California. She is thinking of migrating to Virginia because she has heard that there is a lot of economic development in the northeast megalopolis. You want to encourage her to come.

Write her a letter describing some of the employment opportunities she might find in Virginia.

A Quick Review for YOU!

Answer the following questions:

1. Advances in these two things helped Virginia's economic development:

    A. segregation and integration
    B. transportation and communication
    C. Boston and Hampton Roads

2. Virginia is part of which economies?

    A. state   B. national   C. world   D. A, B, and C

3. Eastern Virginia is part of the:

    A. northeast megalopolis
    B. southwest archaeology dig
    C. Great Plains corn belt

4. Many people from other places in the United States and the world have migrated to Virginia primarily:

    A. to swim at the beach   B. to find a good job
    C. to ride the train   D. to visit friends

5. Match the following:

    1. raw materials   A. go to market
    2. finished goods   B. go to manufacturing centers

And One More for Fun!

ships   poultry   textiles   computer   coal   tourism

Using the word bank above, complete the blanks in the paragraph below!

1. I have a busy family! My Dad works in Norfolk building _____.
2. My Mom is a guide at Williamsburg; she works in the _____ industry.
3. My older brother makes chips (no, not out of potatoes!) at a _____ plant in Arlington.
4. My aunt operates a _____ farm in the Shenandoah Valley.
5. My cousin spent the summer underground at a southwest Virginia _____ mine.
6. My other cousin lives in Danville. She creates patterns for fabrics; she works in Virginia's _____ industry.

I wonder what I will be when I grow up!

Look on the page listed and find the answer to each question.

1. Virginia was one of the _____ original states. (p. 29)

2. Virginia is divided into _____ geographic regions. (p. 50)

3. The House of _____ was the first representative government. (p. 70)

4. The Tidewater and Piedmont regions are separated by a _____ _____. (p. 42)

5. Woodrow Wilson was the _____ President of the United States. (p. 138)

4.6d - Money, banking, saving, and credit play an important role in contemporary Virginia.

Money, Honey, If You Want to Get Along With Me!

Money is not so important for what it is, but for what it can do. Money is the medium of exchange used to purchase goods and services.

The role of money in Virginia today is very important. While early Virginians used barter and trade, today money gives us a more convenient and **acceptable** tool to use instead.

There are three forms of money:

Coins   Currency (Cash)   Checks

Check which medium of exchange you would most likely use to purchase the following goods or services:

	Coins	Cash	Checks
A new winter coat	☐	☐	☐
A candy bar from a vending machine	☐	☐	☐
A lunch at school	☐	☐	☐
A refrigerator	☐	☐	☐
A haircut	☐	☐	☐
A newspaper	☐	☐	☐
A visit to the doctor	☐	☐	☐

Credit is borrowing money (buying now and paying later). Credit is commonly used to purchase goods and services.

We can get credit as: credit cards   loans (usually from banks)

Check which way you might most likely pay for the following goods or services:

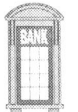

	credit cards	bank loan	cash
A new home	☐	☐	☐
A new car	☐	☐	☐
A school uniform	☐	☐	☐
Weekly groceries	☐	☐	☐
College textbooks	☐	☐	☐
A vacation trip	☐	☐	☐

Virginia's Banks

Banks in Virginia provide essential financial services. Some of the services that banks provide include:

- They lend money to consumers to purchase goods and services such as houses, cars, and education.
- They lend money to producers who start new businesses.
- They issue credit cards.
- They provide savings accounts and pay interest to savers.
- They provide checking accounts.

Check whether you have more, less, or the same amount of money after each of the following events:

You deposit your paycheck into your checking account.	MORE	LESS	SAME
You put $1,000 in a savings account.	MORE	LESS	SAME
You use your credit card to buy new school clothes.	MORE	LESS	SAME
You borrow money from the bank to open a toy store.	MORE	LESS	SAME
You write a check at the grocery store.	MORE	LESS	SAME
You transfer money from checking to savings.	MORE	LESS	SAME

Number the events in the correct order for the situation below:

1. Before you can buy a new car, you must:
    ___ A. save some money
    ___ B. get a job
    ___ C. get a paycheck

Circle ALL the correct answers for the following questions:

2. When you buy something with a credit card:
    A. you may owe interest
    B. you are not responsible for the purchase
    C. you should only spend what you can afford

3. When you write a check:
    A. you get paid interest
    B. you are saving money
    C. it is the same as paying cash

A Quick Review for YOU!

1. Money is a:

   A. financial service
   B. medium of exchange
   C. good or service

2. Credit is:

   A. paying now and buying later
   B. buying now and paying later

3. When you borrow money, you:

   A. owe interest
   B. earn interest

4. When you save money in a savings account, you:

   A. owe interest
   B. earn interest

5. Credit is commonly used to purchase:

   A. daily needs
   B. rent
   C. goods and services

And One More for Fun!

You worked hard this summer. You earned $500! Decide how you will spend it below.

Total Earned: $500.00

I will pay back my Mom this much for money
I borrowed when I first started working: A. $20.00

(subtract A ($20.00) from 500): B._____

I will give my little brother this much money for
taking my phone messages while I was at work: C. $10.00

(subtract C ($10.00) from answer B): D._____

I will spend this much on a special
treat or reward for myself. E. $25.00

(subtract E ($25.00) from answer D): F._____

I will save this much for college. G. $300.00

(subtract G ($300.00) from answer F): H._____

I will put this much in my new savings
account so I can buy school clothes: I. $100.00

(subtract I ($100.00) from answer H): J._____

Total Still Available (*put answer J*): _____

Total Spent (*Add A ($20.00), C ($10.00), and E ($25.00)*): _____

Total Earning Interest and "Growing" My Money!: _____
(Add G ($300.00) and I ($100.00))

4.6e - Different levels of Virginia government collect different types of taxes which are used to provide services to citizens.

A Taxing Matter

Taxes are collected by the government to pay for services. Different tax-supported services are provided by different types of governments.

Your local government may collect ***property tax***. These taxes may be used to build public schools and public libraries, build and repair streets and roads, and pay for police and fire departments.

State governments often collect ***sales tax*** and ***income tax***. They may use these taxes to build state colleges and universities, construct state highways, and give aid to local schools.

The federal government collects ***excise tax***. This is a tax paid on items such as cigarettes and gasoline. The federal government also collects income tax. This is a percentage of the wages you are paid. The federal government uses this tax revenue to build interstate highways and to provide for the national defense.

Match the tax paid with the service it might provide:

1. Sales tax
2. Property tax
3. Excise tax

A. A highway from Virginia to Maryland
B. Books for the new library
C. Teacher salaries at the state college

Put a **P** by the item you would pay Property Tax on.
Put an **S** by the item you would pay Sales Tax on.
Put an **E** by the item you would pay Excise Tax on.
Put an **I** by the item you would pay Income Tax on.

A Quick Review for YOU!

Answer the following questions:

1. Which things might taxes pay for?
    A. schools and libraries
    B. banks
    C. new businesses

2. Taxes are collected by the:
    A. teacher
    B. bank
    C. governor
    D. government

3. Taxes paid to the **federal** government are sometimes used:
    A. To pave local streets and roads
    B. To build state colleges
    C. To provide for the national defense

4. Taxes paid to **local** governments often finance:
    A. interstate highways
    B. police and fire departments
    C. the building of state highways

5. The level of government which uses taxes to pay for colleges and universities is:
    A. local
    B. state
    C. federal

And One More for Fun!

Uh Oh!

*Remember that $500 you made working last summer?
Did you pay taxes on it? If you did, which type of tax did you pay?*

      A. Excise

      B. Income

      C. Property

      D. Sales

Here are some websites to help you learn more about Virginia!

The Virginia Experience! - http://www.virginiaexperience.com

http://www.state.va.us

Virginia Is For Lovers - http://www.virginia.org

Virginia Facts and Figures - http://www.state.va.us/home/facts.html

Life in Colonial Williamsburg - http://www.history.org

Thomas Jefferson - http://www.monticello.org

George Washington - http://www.gwashington1999.org

The American Civil War - http://www.americancivilwar.com

WHERE DO YOUR TAX DOLLARS GO?

Section 3

Extra Credit

Wonderful Words!

Find the words from the Word Bank in the puzzle below.

Word Bank

colony	slaves	Washington
Virginia	tobacco	Monroe
England	barter	freedom
government	Jefferson	Lee
Indians	Wythe	secession

```
E O Q J E F F E R S O N N P R
R C O W B O Z M O D E E R F I
A L K J S C B E R T Y W Q X Y
Q I C O T O B A C C O E R B N
L N I Q X L W D R U Y V Z Q T
I D B P T O C N L T U W C B N
V I R G I N I A O E E C O M Q
I A O X C Y R L Z W O R B O I
C N Q W O T M G O P Y U M N E
C S G O V E R N M E N T U R Z
C O L A S D O E M O P W H O Q
C P W A S H I N G T O N M E I
O W E I V O E V C X Z Y U I O
Z O V L E E X W Y Z R T S D F
N B C O E X S E C E S S I O N
```

More Wonderful Words!

Imagine that you are writing a letter to someone who has never been to Virginia. Fill in the blanks with your own words.

Dear _____,

Please come visit me in Virginia! I think you would have a lot of fun visiting _____ (my town). Since I live in the _____ Region, we would find _____ and _____ nearby. My favorite time of year in Virginia is _____ (season), because _____. If you want to travel around the state, we could visit _____ and _____ (places I've been before).

Sincerely,

_____

Tumultuous Timelines!

Put the following events in the correct sequence on the timeline below by numbering them.

1600

[ ] ERA OF MASSIVE RESISTANCE.

[ ] DECLARATION OF INDEPENDENCE WRITTEN

[ ] CONSTITUTIONAL CONVENTION

[ ] SETTLING OF JAMESTOWN

[ ] CHARTERS OF THE VIRGINIA COMPANY OF LONDON

[ ] WILLIAMSBURG BECOMES THE COLONIAL CAPITAL

[ ] FIRST REPRESENTATIVE ASSEMBLY IN THE NEW WORLD

[ ] CIVIL WAR BEGINS

[ ] CIVIL WAR ENDS - SLAVES ARE FREED

[ ] RICHMOND BECOMES VIRGINIA'S CAPITAL

[ ] FIRST BLACK GOVERNOR ELECTED IN VIRGINIA

PRESENT

Scavenger Hunt!

Use the information on the listed pages to find the answers to these questions. . .

Page #	Question
10	What group of Indians lived in the Piedmont region?
12	Where did the Scottish, Irish, and Germans settle?
20	Write the name of a city that developed around the Chesapeake Bay:
21	Why did cities grow up along the fall line?
36	What type of industry is found in Northern Virginia?
39	What is the main industry on the Eastern Shore?
46	On what river is Hampton Roads located?
53	What does the word "Shenandoah" mean?
71	Why did conflict develop between the colonies and England?
76	What is a mob cap?

Early American Food Trivia

Below are some foods that Virginians ate long ago (and still eat today — but some are not named the same). Can you match the food with its definition?

1. Succotash _____
2. Marmalade _____
3. Fool _____
4. Shoofly Pie _____
5. Punch _____
6. Spoon bread _____
7. Hoppin' John _____
8. Salat _____
9. Apoquinimine Cakes _____
10. Pone _____
11. Chowder _____
12. Red-eye gravy _____
13. Cider _____
14. Ham Hock _____

A. a form of beaten biscuits

B. a thick soup made with clams, fish and vegetables

C. pan gravy made from fried ham

D. juice made from apples or other fruit

E. ankle of a pig

F. a loaf or oval-shaped bread or cake

G. salad

H. a dish made with black-eyed peas, rice, and salt pork or bacon

I. a dish made of corn and beans

J. a baked dish made of cornmeal, eggs, and shortening

K. jelly or preserves with small pieces of fruit or rind in it

L. an English dessert made of crushed, cooked fruit and cream or custard

M. pie filled with a mixture of flour, butter, brown sugar, and molasses

N. a drink made with two or more fruit juices, sugar, spices, and water

What Did You Sayeth?!

Below are some Old English words that Virginians spoke long ago. Write a short story using some of these words . . .

Arn - iron • Balloo - a game of ball • Costardmonger - apple seller
Crevise - lobster • Dibble - moustache • Frumety - oatmeal
Luzarne - bobcat or mountain lion
Mammothrept - spoiled child • Openauk - potato
Piddle-diddle - procrastinate • Seekanauk - king or horseshoe crab
Shot Sharks - underwear • Strummel Patched - long, loose, tangled hair
Weroance - Indian chief

Fill-In Crossword

Let's visit the regions again! Fill in the blank crossword with the names of the four regions and their unique characteristics. We've given you one to start from.

Allegheny Appalachian Plateau
Coal mines

Ridge and Valley
Blue Ridge Mountains
Shenandoah

Piedmont
Peanuts
Tobacco

Tidewater
Eastern Shore

4th & 5th Grade Practice Test

1. In which region did the Powhatan Indians live?
    A. Piedmont Region
    B. Tidewater Region
    C. Ridge and Valley Region
    D. Allegheny (Appalachian) Plateau

2. Where did the Scotch, Irish, and Germans settle?
    A. near the James River
    B. near the Pacific Ocean
    C. in the Shenandoah Valley
    D. in the Blue Ridge Mountains

3. Which of these cities developed at the mouth of the Chesapeake Bay?
    A. Richmond
    B. Alexandria
    C. Roanoke
    D. Norfolk

4. On what river was Richmond founded?
    A. the Potomac River
    B. the James River
    C. the Chesapeake River
    D. the New River

5. Which of the following states does not form part of Virginia's border?
    A. Texas
    B. West Virginia
    C. Kentucky
    D. North Carolina

6. Which industry became important in the Tidewater region?
    A. Lumbering
    B. Coal mining
    C. Poultry farming
    D. Shipping

7. In what region is coal mined?
    A. Allegheny (Appalachian) Plateau
    B. Ridge and Valley
    C. Piedmont
    D. Tidewater

8. Which of these areas has low population density?
    A. Richmond
    B. Northern Virginia
    C. Eastern Shore
    D. Virginia Beach

9. In what region are the Blue Ridge Mountains located?
    A. Tidewater
    B. Ridge and Valley
    C. Piedmont
    D. Allegheny (Appalachian) Plateau

10. Into how many regions is the United States divided?
    A. four
    B. five
    C. six
    D. seven

11. Which of the following was the first representative assembly in America?
    A. Congress
    B. General Court
    C. House of Burgesses
    D. House of Representatives

12. What type of government did the Virginia colony have?
    A. representative
    B. monarchy
    C. communist
    D. socialist

13. Which of the following groups did *not* contribute to the development of the Virginia colony?
    A. German settlers
    B. migrant workers
    C. African slaves
    D. American Indians

14. How did colonists buy goods and services in colonial Virginia?
    A. They bartered
    B. They used coins
    C. They wrote checks
    D. They used credit cards

15. Which of the following was not a reason for the start of the Civil War?
    A. The color of the national flag
    B. States' rights
    C. Slavery
    D. The preservation of the Union

16. Who commanded the Confederate Army?
    A. Ulysses S. Grant
    B. Jefferson Davis
    C. Thomas Jackson
    D. Robert E. Lee

17. What were the years after the Civil War called?
    A. Massive Resistance
    B. Reconstruction
    C. Rebuilding Time
    D. Civil Rights Era

18. What were the laws that discriminated against African-Americans called?
    A. John Doe laws
    B. Equal Rights laws
    C. Jim Crow laws
    D. Integration laws

19. What happened to Virginia's cities after Reconstruction?
    A. They became more violent
    B. They became less safe
    C. They got smaller
    D. They began to grow

20. Which of the following is *not* a type of service provided by the government?
    A. Massages
    B. Public schools
    C. Police and fire departments
    D. Interstate highways

Section 4

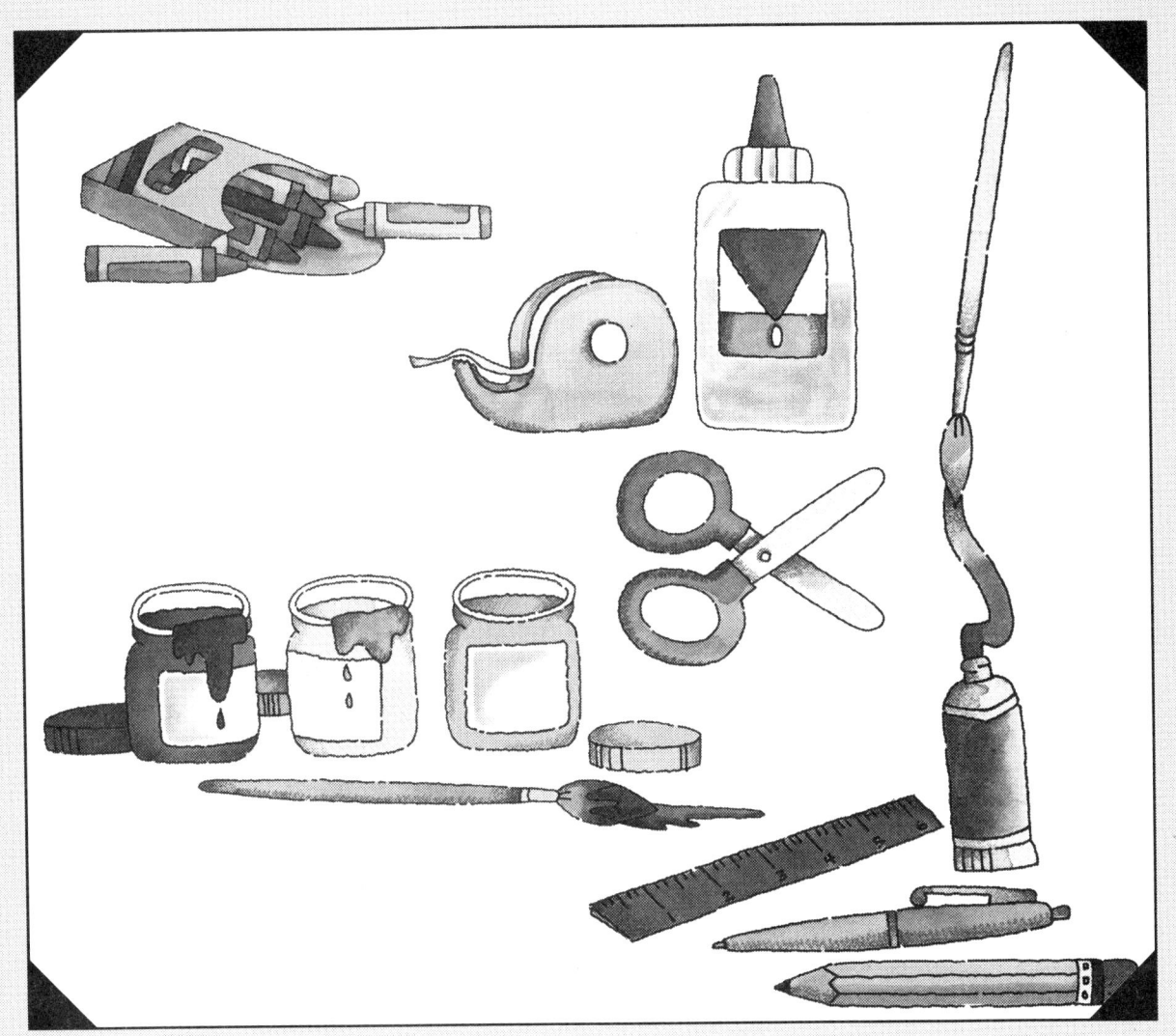

Appendix

VIRGINIA

~ 9500 BC — Paleo (ancient) people inhabit Virginia

1492 AD — Christopher Columbus discovers America

1607 — 104 English colonists establish a settlement at Jamestown

1619 — House of Burgesses formed; first Africans brought to Virginia

1624 — Virginia becomes a royal British colony

1644 — Peace treaty with Powhatan Indians signed

1649 — Slavery practiced in Virginia

1676 — Nathaniel Bacon's Rebellion against the governor

1693 — College of William and Mary chartered

1699 — Capital moved to Williamsburg (Middle Plantation)

1775 — Revolutionary War begins

1776 — Declaration of Independence from England signed

1780 — Richmond becomes capital

1781 — British surrender at Yorktown

1786 — Virginia Statute for Religious Freedom adopted

1788 — Virginia becomes the 10th American state

1789 — George Washington becomes first U.S. president

1800 — Slave Gabriel leads revolt

TIMELINE

1801 — Thomas Jefferson becomes America's third president

1831 — Nat Turner's Rebellion against slavery

1859 — John Brown raids Harpers Ferry

1861 — Virginia secedes from the Union; Civil War starts

1865 — Robert E. Lee surrenders at Appomattox; Civil War ends

1870 — Virginia readmitted to the Union

1914 — Virginians serve in World War I

1920 — Virginia women get the right to vote

1941 — Virginians serve in World War II

1959 — Virginia schools begin to integrate

1964 — Civil Rights Act passed

1965 — Virginians serve in Vietnam War

1988 — Virginia celebrates its bicentennial

1989 — Virginia elects first African-American governor in the nation, L. Douglas Wilder

1999 — Virginia students on the Internet

2001 — Virginia enters the 21st Century

WHAT IS IN VIRGINIA'S FUTURE??

People

Colonial and Revolutionary War Eras

Nathaniel Bacon, a young plantation owner, led a rebellion against the colonial government in Virginia in 1676. He claimed the government did not protect farmers from Indian raids, led other farmers in attacks against the Indians, and captured and burned the city of Jamestown.

George Rogers Clark, a Revolutionary War soldier born near Charlottesville, helped win battles which extended U.S. territories far to the west.

William Clark was born in Caroline County. He was part of the expedition that included Meriwether Lewis and was sent to explore the Louisiana Territory.

"I have not yet begun to fight!" cried **John Paul Jones**, a Fredericksburg naval officer, when the British demanded he surrender during a 1779 Revolutionary War battle.

Francis Lightfoot Lee, Richard Henry Lee's brother, was a member of the House of Burgesses, signed the Declaration of Independence, and was a delegate to the First Continental Congress.

"Light-Horse Harry" Lee, born near Dumfries, was a great cavalry commander during the American Revolution. He was a member of the Continental Congress, served as governor of Virginia and a member of the House of Representatives.

Richard Henry Lee was a political leader in colonial Virginia. He signed the Declaration of Independence, served in the Continental Congress, and was a U.S. Senator.

Meriwether Lewis, born in Albemarle County, explored the Louisiana Purchase with William Clark.

Much legend has grown up around the life of the Indian princess **Pocahontas**. The fact is that she was the daughter of the Indian chief Powhatan when the first settlers came to Virginia. She was the first Indian in the New World converted to Christianity, married John Rolfe, and traveled with him to England. Sadly, she died when she was only 22 years old.

Even less is known about **Chief Powhatan** than his legendary daughter. It is said that he ruled over about 9,000 Indians in what is now eastern Virginia. He tried to keep the peace with the English settlers, but it must have been difficult for him to see his people's native lands gradually taken away by the white colonists. After he died, relations between the Indians and whites grew worse until the Indians were completely forced off their lands.

Without the efforts of **Sir Walter Raleigh**, Virginia may never have been settled. He organized several voyages to the New World, including the famous Lost Colony. He gave Virginia its name but never set foot on its shores himself.

The husband of the Indian princess Pocahontas, **John Rolfe**, made an important contribution to Virginia's future by developing a sweeter-smelling tobacco that was popular in England. Without this cash crop, Virginia would not have become a leading British colony and the successful state it is today.

Without **Captain John Smith**, the Jamestown colony would not have survived. As a member of the first group of settlers, he tried to get along with the Indians, even learning their language. He forced the settlers to work hard and spent a lot of time exploring and mapping the Atlantic coast.

Civil War Era

An ardent abolitionist, **John Brown** led a raid on Harpers Ferry (now part of West Virginia) in 1859 in an attempt to free the slaves through armed force. His raid was stopped by the U.S. military, but it had the effect of increasing tension between the North and the South before the Civil War.

One of the greatest and most famous Confederate Civil War generals, **Thomas Jackson**, was born in Clarksburg and nicknamed "Stonewall" for his firm stance during battle.

Born a slave in Southampton County, **Nat Turner** led a slave rebellion in 1831 where nearly 60 people were killed. The rebellion led to stricter slave codes in the South.

Musical Virginians

Pearl Bailey was born in Newport News. As a singer and actress, she won a Tony Award and was a frequent guest at the White House. She won the Medal of Freedom in 1988 for her commitment to her country.

Alvin Pleasant Carter, born in Maces Spring, formed the Carter Family singers, who recorded more than 300 mountain, folk, and country music songs.

Patsy Cline was born in Gore during the Great Depression. She was the first female country singer to break into the pop music charts. Two of her best-known hits are *I Fall to Pieces* and *Crazy*.

Ella Fitzgerald, born in Newport News, was the first female singer to develop a jazz-style voice. She became famous for singing in a "scat" style and performed all over the world with well-known musicians.

Bill "Bojangles" Robinson, born in Richmond, is honored each year with National Tap Dance Day.

Kate Smith of Greenville became known as the "first lady of radio" and was famous for singing "God Bless America."

Soprano **Camilla Williams**, from Danville, was the first African-American to sing a major role at the Vienna State Opera, in 1954, in Madame Butterfly.

Scientific Virginians

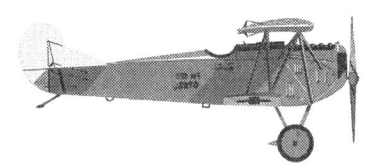

Richard Byrd, born in Winchester, was one of the first two people to fly over the North Pole in 1926. He later explored the Arctic and Antarctic.

Hampton's **Katherine Johnson**, a mathematician and NASA scientist, used pencil and paper to do the algebra for the Alan Shepard flight, the John Glenn orbit, and the 1969 Apollo moon mission.

Sarah Garland Jones was the first African-American and the first woman to be certified by the Virginia State Board of Medicine. In 1895, she and her husband co-founded Richmond Community Hospital.

Inventor of the reaper, **Cyrus McCormick** of Rockbridge County helped revolutionize farming in Virginia and the nation!

Belroi-born **Walter Reed** was an army doctor who helped save lives when he discovered how the diseases typhoid and yellow fever were spread through mosquito bites!

Booker T. Washington, born near Roanoke, helped Tuskegee Institute to become a leading center of black education.

Carter G. Woodson, born in Buckingham County in 1875, founded Negro History Week, now Black History Month, to celebrate the achievements of African-Americans.

Political Virginians

William Henry Harrison, born in Charles City County, was the 9th President. He died of pneumonia after serving only one month in office.

George Marshall of Uniontown was awarded the 1953 Nobel Peace Prize for his role in helping to rebuild Europe after World War II.

Judge **John Marshall**, born near Germantown (now Midland), helped build the U.S. Supreme Court into a strong and equal branch of the federal government.

Zachary Taylor, born in Orange County, was the 12th president of the U.S. He was known as "Old Rough and Ready."

John Tyler was William Henry Harrison's vice-president and took over the presidency after Harrison's death. He was born in Charles City County and served as governor of Virginia and a U.S. senator before becoming vice-president.

Literary Virginians

Anne Beattie, a resident of Charlottesville, has won numerous awards and distinctions for her early stories published in *New Yorker* and her subsequent novels.

Willa Cather, born near Winchester, is best known for her novels, *O Pioneers!* and *My Antonia*, which she wrote based on her experiences migrating west with her family.

Virginius Dabney was an award-winning editor of the *Ricmond Times-Dispatch* from 1936–1969.

Contemporary author **Annie Dillard** received a Pulitzer Prize in 1975 for *Pilgrim at Tinker Creek*, about life in the Roanoke River Valley.

With little formal education but by being a voracious reader, **Ellen Glasgow** became such an excellent writer about Virginia that her book, *In This Our Life*, won a Pulitzer Prize in 1942.

Many young Americans learned to read from **William McGuffey's** "Readers" in the late 1800s and early 1900s.

Edgar Allan Poe, raised in Richmond, was a popular short story writer who is still read by people who want a good scare!

Athletic Virginians

Eppa Rixey, born in Culpeper in 1891, was the first Virginian elected to the Baseball Hall of Fame, in 1963. He pitched in 21 seasons and won 266 games for the Philadelphia Phillies and the Cincinnati Reds from 1912 through 1933.

Hot Springs' **Sam Snead** was a hot pro golfer, winning more than 100 tournaments, some on the world's most challenging links!

Piratical Virginians?

Known as "the fiercest pirate of them all," **Blackbeard** (real name: Ned Teach, Edward Thatch, or something similar) was once a regular visitor to Virginia's shores. After he was caught and decapitated, his head was hung on a pole along the Hampton River, at a place called Blackbeard's Point.

Virginia Basic Facts

Nicknames: Old Dominion, Mother of Presidents, Mother of States
State Motto: Sic Semper Tyrannis (Thus Always to Tyrants)
Area: 42,326 square miles; 35th in the nation

Virginia — Old Dominion

Record low temperature: -30° F (-34° C) at Mountain Lake Bio Station

Record high temperature: 110° F (43° C) at Columbia

State Insect: Tiger Swallowtail Butterfly

State Tree: Flowering dogwood

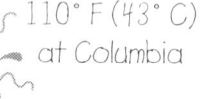

State Bird: Cardinal

State Dog: American foxhound

State Capital: Richmond

State Flower: Dogwood

Highest Elevation: Mount Rogers, 5,729 feet (1,746 meters)

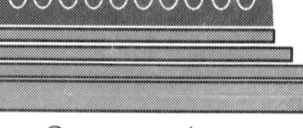

Lowest Elevation: Sea Level

State Shell: Oyster

State Fish: Brook trout

State Drink: Milk

Government: 2 U.S. senators, 11 U.S. representatives.

Legislative body: General Assembly – 40 senators, 100 representatives. 95 counties.

©2000 Carole Marsh/Gallopade International • 800-536-2GET • www.virginiaexperience.com
~ This book is not reproducible. ~

Gazetteer

This page will help you find the places mentioned in the Fourth Grade Student Workbook.

Allegheny (Appalachian) Plateau: found in the southwestern corner of Virginia; consists of a plateau and valuable coal deposits.

Appalachian Mountains: low, rounded mountains that run along the western edge of Virginia.

Atlantic Ocean: the large body of water that borders the United States on the east.

Chesapeake Bay: body of water that separates the mainland of Virginia from the Eastern Shore.

Delmarva Peninsula: peninsula formed by Delaware, part of Maryland, and the Eastern Shore of Virginia.

Eastern Shore: a peninsula east of mainland Virginia.

Great Dismal Swamp: large swamp found in southeastern Virginia extending into North Carolina.

Hampton Roads: harbor area formed at the mouth of the James River.

James River: the longest river wholly within Virginia; runs from the mountains to Hampton Roads.

Jamestown: located on a peninsula on the James River, about 34 miles from the mouth of the river.

Lake Drummond: found in the Great Dismal Swamp, it is the largest natural lake in Virginia.

Piedmont Region: the region next to the Tidewater region; contains a plateau, rolling hills, rapids, and a fall line.

Potomac River: forms the boundary between Virginia and Maryland.

Richmond: capital city of Virginia; on the fall line and the James River.

Ridge and Valley Region: contains the Blue Ridge Mountains, valleys, caverns, and the Shenandoah River.

Shenandoah Valley: valley formed by the Shenandoah River; runs between the Shenandoah and Blue Ridge mountains.

Tidewater Region: the region of Virginia next to the Atlantic Ocean; a coastal plain.

Williamsburg: second colonial capital of Virginia, located near Jamestown.

Geography Glossary

bay: a part of an ocean, sea, or lake that extends into the land.

canal: a waterway built to carry water for navigation or irrigation.

cavern: a large cave or natural opening into or under the earth.

coast: the land along an ocean or sea.

community: a group of people who live in a specific place, share government, and often have a common history.

English: people who live in or come from the country of England.

European: people who live in or come from the continent of Europe.

fall line: the natural boundary between the Piedmont and Coastal Plain regions.

harbor: a part of a body of water deep enough to anchor a ship.

hill: a rounded, raised landform, that is not as high as a mountain.

lake: a body of water completely or almost completely surrounded by land.

latitude: imaginary lines which run horizontally (east and west) around the globe (also called parallels).

longitude: imaginary lines which run vertically (north and south) around the globe.

mountain: a high, rounded, or pointed landform with steep sides.

mountain range: a row or chain of mountains.

natural resources: things that exist in or are formed by nature.

ocean: one of the earth's four largest bodies of salt water.

orchard: a grove of trees which bear fruit.

peninsula: a body of land surrounded on three sides by water.

plateau: a high land area with a flat top.

population density: the average number of people who live in a square mile of land.

poultry: chickens, turkeys, ducks, or geese raised for their meat or eggs.

rapids: a part of a river where the water flows swiftly and roughly.

river: a large stream of water that flows in a natural channel across the land and empties into a lake, ocean, or another river.

river mouth: the place where a river empties into a larger body of water.

temperate: mild; neither too hot, nor too cold.

tributary: a river or stream that flows into a larger river or stream.

valley: a long, narrow piece of low land set between mountains or hills.

History Glossary

abolition: to do away with something; abolitionists wanted to do away with slavery.

barter: to trade one thing for another.

charter: a document issued by a government authority.

colony: a group of people who leave their native country to form a settlement in a new land.

compromise: to settle differences by each side giving up something to the other side.

conflict: a fight, battle, or struggle.

consumer: a buyer of goods or services.

credit: getting something today that you promise to pay for at a later time.

debt: something that you owe to someone else.

guarantee: to promise, assure, or pledge.

patriot: a person who loves, serves, and defends his or her country.

resign: to give up or quit, as in to quit your job.

secession: to pull away from; to leave.

surrender: to give up, as in to give up to an enemy force.

statute: a formal rule enacted by a legislature.

Glossary of Indian Words and Names

Algonquian (al-gahn-kwee-uhn): language spoken by the Powhatans in Virginia and related to other Indian languages along the Atlantic coast.

Cattapeuk: meant "spring."

Chesapeake (ches-a-peak): means "big salt bay."

Chickahominy (chick-a-hom-a-nee): means "crushed corn people."

Cohattayough: meant "summer."

huskanaw: Powhatan initiation into manhood.

mamanatowick: title given to the chief Powhatan.

Okeus: the Powhatans' most powerful god.

Opechancanough: Powhatan's brother, who became weroance after Powhatan's death in 1618.

pawcorances: altar stones which stood by people's homes, out in the woods, or at any spot that was significant.

peak: a type of bead made from quahog shells used by the Powhatans in trading; also called wampum.

Popanow: meant "winter."

Pocahontas (poh-kuh-hahn-tuhs): Daughter of the chief Powhatan, her name means "little playful one." Also called Matoaka.

Powhatan (pow-a-tan): name for 1) a chief's empire that covered most of the Virginia coastal plain; 2) the name of the chief of a group of Indians; 3) the name of the town where Powhatan was born, near the falls of the James River. May mean "priest's town" or "town at the falls."

weroance: name given to Powhatan's "commanders," or sub-chiefs.

yihakan (yeee-ha-cahn): a Powhatan house.

Reference Guide

If you need to get more basic information about Virginia's history, government, economy, etc., here are some good books for you to check out of the library.

America the Beautiful: Virginia, by Sylvia McNair. Childrens Press, 1989.

From Sea to Shining Sea: Virginia, by Dennis B. Fradin. Childrens Press, 1992.

Hello U.S.A.: Virginia, by Karen Sirvaitis. Lerner Publications Company, 1991.

Let's Discover the States, ATLANTIC, District of Columbia• Virginia• West Virginia, by Thomas G. Aylesworth and Virginia L. Aylesworth. Chelsea House Publishers, 1988.

My First Book About Virginia!, by Carole Marsh. Gallopade International, 1998.

Steck-Vaughn Portrait of America: Virginia, by Kathleen Thompson. Steck-Vaughn Company, 1996.

The Virginia Experience, by Carole Marsh. Gallopade International, 2000.

A Map of North America

A Map of the United States

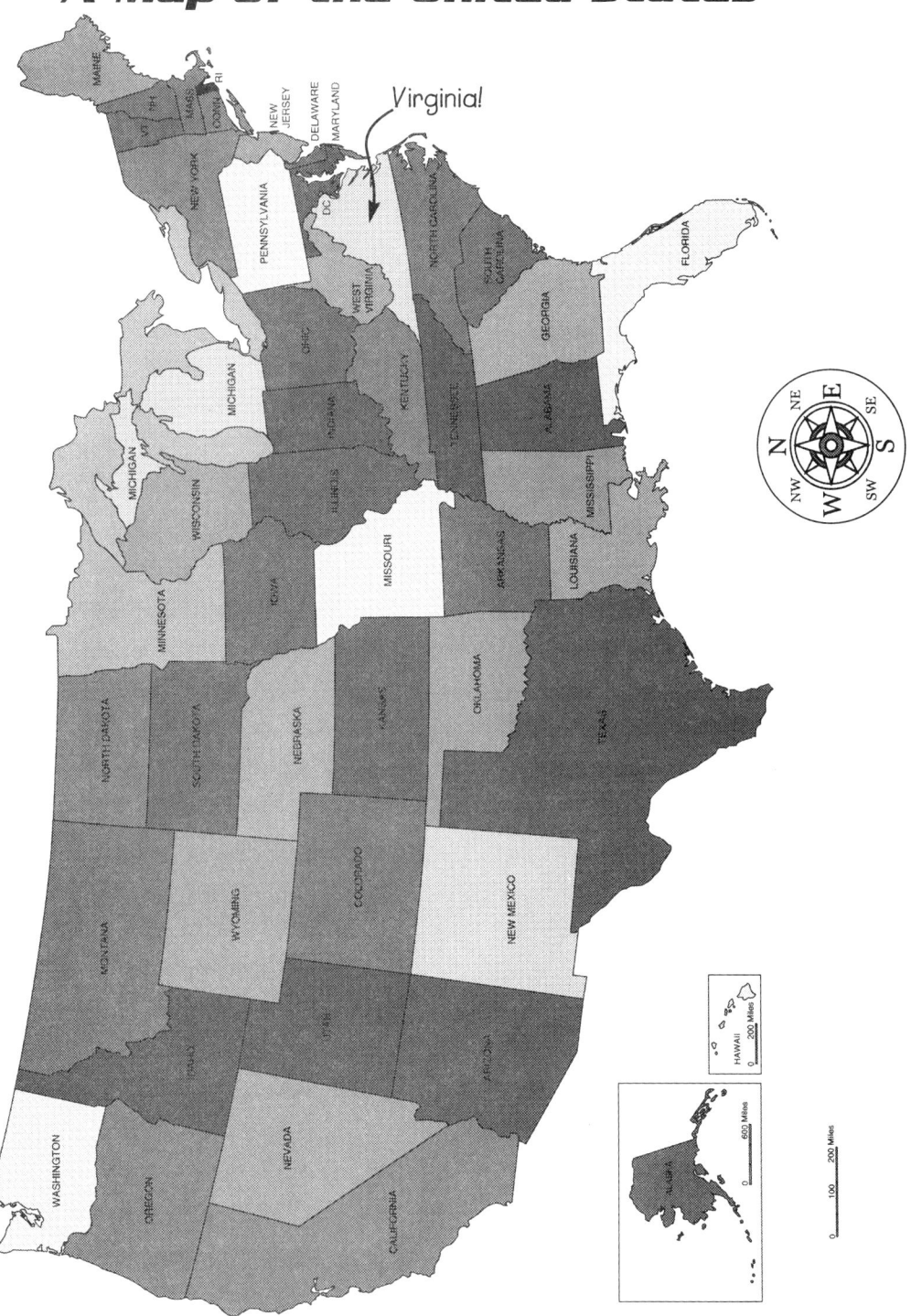

A Map of the 13 Colonies

THE UNITED STATES, 1787

- New Hampshire
- New York
- Massachusetts
- Pennsylvania
- Rhode Island
- Connecticut
- New Jersey
- Delaware
- Maryland
- Virginia
- North Carolina
- South Carolina
- Georgia

U.S. Territory (Northwest)

U.S. Territory

MISSISSIPPI RIVER

OHIO RIVER

Virginia's Major Cities

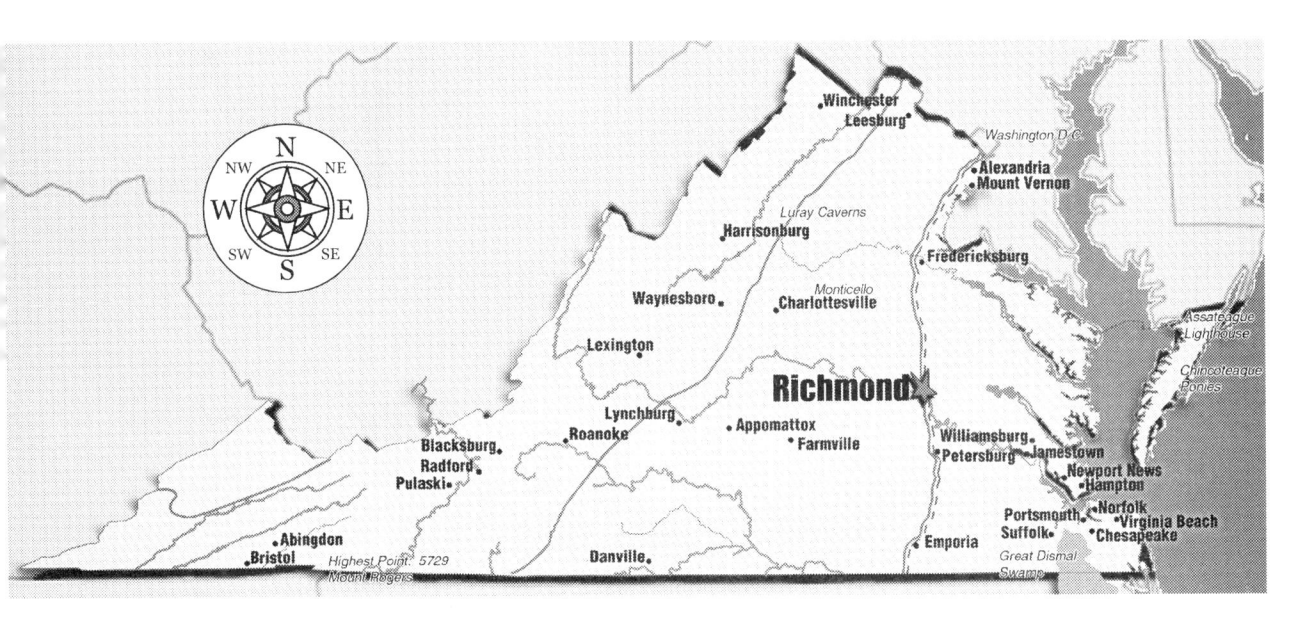

Virginia's Rivers & Mountains

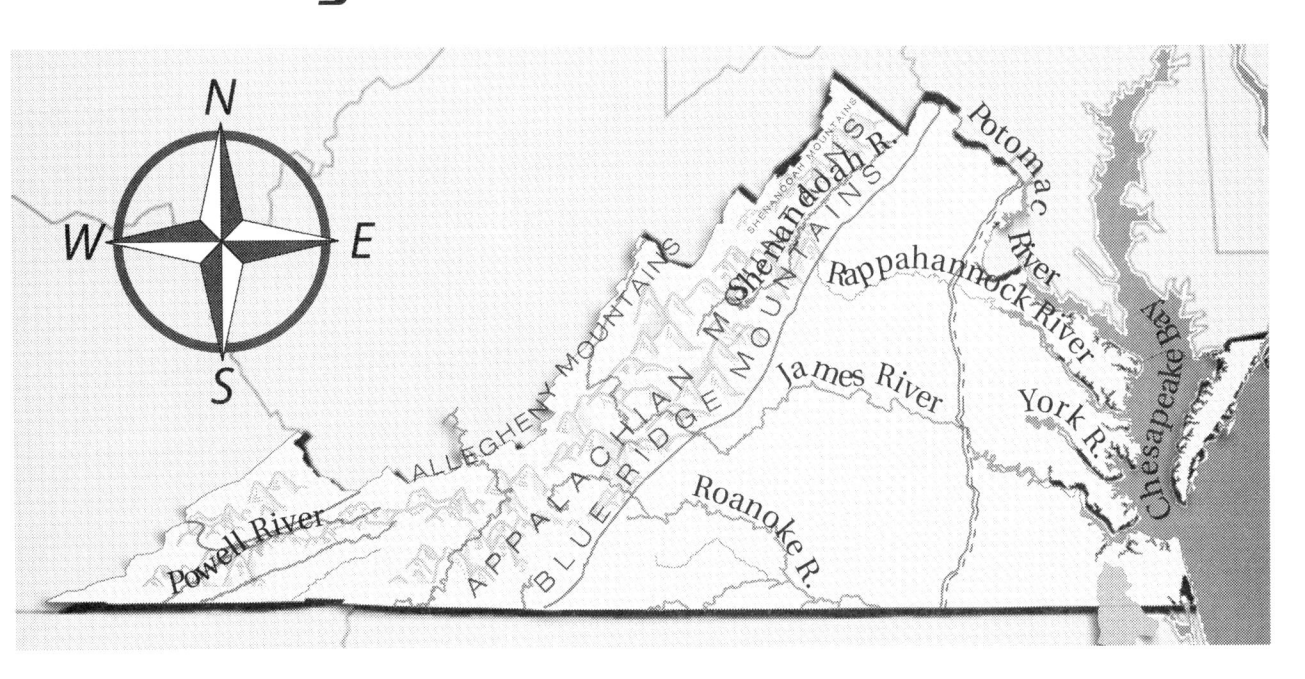

Index

Abraham Lincoln 118, 119
absolute location 25
Africa 14, 30, 80, 84, 97, 130, 138, 140, 141, 172, 173, 177, 178
Alexandria 21, 42
Allegheny (Appalachian) Plateau 10, 34, 50, 54, 181
American Revolution 92, 96, 174. See also Revolutionary War.
architecture 39, 43, 72, 75
Arthur Ashe 138
Atlantic Ocean 19, 27, 30, 52, 57, 58, 181

banks 89, 90, 151, 152
barter 87, 89, 150, 183
Bill of Rights 101, 103, 106, 112
Blue Ridge Mountains 52, 53, 84, 181
Bull Run 121, 122

cardinal directions 24
caverns 44, 53, 181
Chesapeake Bay 19, 20, 33, 51, 181
Civil Rights Act 173
Civil Rights Movement 140
Civil War 119, 121, 122, 123, 126, 159, 164, 173, 176
coal 34, 35, 45, 54, 133, 143, 181
compass rose 24
credit 87, 88, 89, 150, 151, 152, 183
culture 72

Danville 36, 177
Declaration of Independence 94, 95, 100, 101, 106, 107, 164, 172, 174, 175

Eastern Shore 39, 74, 181
Economic Interdependence 67
England 11, 66, 67, 68, 69, 71, 72, 73, 75, 76, 83, 84, 89, 92, 93, 94, 95, 104, 107, 172, 175, 176, 182
Europe 11, 29, 178, 182

fall line 21, 41, 42, 51, 52, 181, 182
fashion 72, 76, 84
Freedman's Bureau 127
French and Indian War 71, 72, 93

General Assembly 70, 180
geographic location 26
George Mason 65, 103, 112
George Washington 65, 72, 100, 112, 113, 159, 172
Germans 12, 80, 84
grid system 25

Hampton 20, 177
Hampton Roads 46, 145, 146, 181
harbor 11, 20, 33, 46, 119, 181, 182
Harrisonburg 22
Harry F. Byrd 138
House of Burgesses 70, 82, 95, 100, 103, 172, 174

Indentured servants 82, 90
Irish 12, 80, 84

J.E.B. Stuart 122
James Madison 101, 112, 113, 115
James Monroe 102, 113
James River 11, 21, 41, 46, 51, 52, 181, 184
Jamestown 10, 11, 72, 164, 172, 174, 176, 181
Jim Crow laws 130
John Brown 118, 173, 176
John Rolfe 84, 175, 176

L. Douglas Wilder 138, 173
language 10, 72, 74, 176, 184
latitude 26, 182
legend 24
longitude 26, 182
Louisiana Purchase 101, 102, 113, 175

Manassas 121
map key 24
Massive Resistance 138, 140, 141, 164
megalopolis 145

Nat Turner 118, 173, 176
natural resources 11, 20, 33, 89, 182
Norfolk 20, 33
Northern Virginia 36, 43, 137, 146

Patrick Henry 65, 103, 104
peninsula 39, 181, 182
Piedmont 10, 34, 50, 52, 181, 182
plantation 14, 83, 90, 118, 127, 172, 174
population density 39, 40, 41, 43, 182
Portsmouth 33
Potomac River 21, 27, 43, 51, 181
Powhatan 10, 172, 175, 184

Reconstruction 126, 130, 133
relative location 27
religion 72, 73, 106, 112
representative government 69, 70
Revolutionary War 65, 96, 97, 116, 174. See also American Revolution.
Richmond 21, 25, 26, 41, 42, 119, 121, 125, 138, 164, 172, 177, 179, 180, 181
Ridge and Valley 34, 50, 53, 181
Robert E. Lee 122, 173

Scottish 12
Segregation 130, 140, 141
Separate but equal 141
Shenandoah River 44, 53, 181
Shenandoah Valley 12, 22, 44, 181
Slaves 14, 30, 80, 84, 90, 95, 117, 118, 126, 127, 164, 176
society 72, 84, 87, 90, 130, 133, 141

taxes 71, 130, 156
Thomas "Stonewall" Jackson 122, 176
Thomas Jefferson 94, 95, 101, 102, 112, 113, 159, 173
Tidewater 10, 14, 33, 34, 50, 51, 74, 181
Tobacco 13, 34, 83, 84, 87, 90, 144, 176
tourism 33, 144
transportation 21, 33, 35, 39, 133, 143

Virginia Company of London 66, 82, 106, 164
Virginia Declaration of Rights 103, 106, 112
Virginia Statute for Religious Freedom 101, 106, 112, 172

Winchester 22, 177, 178
Woodrow Wilson 138

Yorktown 20, 96, 172

About the Author...

CAROLE MARSH has been writing about Virginia for more than 20 years. She is the author of the popular Virginia State Stuff series for young readers and creator, along with her son, Michael Marsh, of "Virginia Facts and Factivities," a CD-ROM widely used in Virginia schools. The Byrd side of her family history led the author to spend a great deal of time researching, writing, and making photographs in Virginia. The author of more than 100 Virginia books and other supplementary educational materials, Marsh is currently working on a new collection of Virginia materials for young people, including a "Virginia Pocket Guide for Kids." Marsh correlates her Virginia materials to Virginia's Standards of Learning. Many of her books and other materials have been inspired by or requested by Virginia teachers and librarians.

Note to Teachers

The Answer Key for this workbook is included in *The Virginia Experience for Fourth Graders and Fifth Grade Review Teacher Resource Book*. If you did not purchase the Teacher Resource Book and need the Answer Key, please call 800-536-2438 and we will fax or mail one to you.